THE TRUTH ABOUT AIR AMERICA AND THE CIA

ALLEN CATES

iUniverse LLC
Bloomington

Honor Denied
The Truth about Air America and the CIA

iUniverse books may be ordered through booksellers or by contacting:

iUniverse LLC
1663 Liberty Drive
Bloomington, IN 47403
www.iuniverse.com
1-800-Authors (1-800-288-4677)

ISBN: 978-1-4620-5746-7 (sc)
ISBN: 978-1-4620-5748-1 (hc)
ISBN: 978-1-4620-5747-4 (e)

Printed in the United States of America

iUniverse rev. date: 03/31/2014

Not a drum was heard, not a funeral note,
As his corse to the rampart we hurried;
Not a soldier discharged his farewell shot
O'er the grave where our hero we buried.

—from *The Burial of Sir John Moore at Corunna*
by Irish Poet Charles Wolfe (1791–1823)

Contents

Preface

I have always been an avid proponent for the preservation of history, and the history of the war in Southeast Asia would not be complete if Air America is excluded. Historical preservation has very little value if it is not accurate.

Seeing does not necessarily foster believing, and being ubiquitous does not always provide enlightenment. Air America, with its silver, white, and blue aircraft, was definitely omnipresent, visible in numerous pictorial events and several documentaries, and observed in every airport, landing field, and mud puddle in Southeast Asia for a quarter of a century. Yet no one really knew who we were, what we did, or why we were there. The military, those who fought that war, often considered Air America to be war profiteers, mercenaries, and misfits who were interfering in *their* war, and there was strong resentment. Books and articles by university professors and columnists described Air America as filled with drug runners and malcontents. Movie spoofs with well-known actors perpetrated the myths, and the government deceitfully encouraged the subterfuge by obscuring the truth in a cloak of secrecy with an ostentatious label.

Film footage by major networks clearly showed Air America aircraft but made no mention of the company itself. Air America's participation in memorable and honorable events was often redacted, or explained off-handedly as ambulance chasing by people who just happened to be in the area without jurisdiction or authority. Years later, authors wrote about the Air America-CIA connection, but it was obvious the reported nexus was meant to offer intrigue, romance, and sensationalism, not historical fact. The CIA was certainly involved, but saying the CIA owned Air America, although it was supposed to explain everything, really divulged nothing. The truth is sealed in a conspiratorial, convoluted, and seemingly impenetrable matrix.

Honor Denied is not intended to be a memoir, because Air America was not about me. I was a line pilot and not extraordinarily different from those others with whom I served. But you can't unravel the tangled web and release the truth about war unless you've heard the sounds of dying, smelled the blood mixed with cordite, and personally looked death in the face—even then, that is not nearly enough. Sometimes, as it has been said, you are so close to the forest that you can't see the trees. Therefore, it took years of research for me to separate the nut from the shell.

I spent eight years in Southeast Asia fighting a war from the cockpit of an airplane and a helicopter. Three of those years were in Vietnam, and the remaining five years were in Laos, first with the Marines and then with Air America. The war in Southeast Asia ended for Air America in 1975. Twenty-five years later, while president of the Air America Association, I was tasked with seeking veteran status for former employees of the company. I spent five years of intensive research learning the history of Air America and discovered that the things I believed were true and what I had been told about the company were essentially false. I knew from firsthand experience there was a military connection, but proving it was more difficult than I imagined. I began to see that the lines between the dots were not always connected, and incredibly, to me at least, I found out the Defense and State departments really did not, and still do not, want the public to know the truth.

Honor Denied is the culmination of this experience and research, specifically describing Air America, what it was, and its purpose. It explains why men, and now women, go to war voluntarily and what they hope to achieve by doing so. It makes clear how many Air America employees were killed in action, and many more wounded and injured with permanent disability, but how honor for these sacrifices was denied. And in so doing, *Honor Denied* tells the truth about a unique organization that deserves more than it received. It is a story that needs to be told, and I am here to tell it.

The Beginning Of A Journey

The word *truth* can have a variety of meanings. The Bible says, "Faith is the substance of things hoped for, and the evidence of things not seen." Kind of hard to argue with that, and truth often falls into the same slot—the interpretation varies widely. For example, saints and sinners alike have used the Bible to corroborate their arguments about what truth is. So it seems to me that truth is often based on who says it, and how naive people are about the subject.

Regardless, in the summer of 1960, standing on the dirt road that led to my parents' house in Southwest Missouri, I found myself staring truth in the face. It was an enlightening experience, but not particularly pleasant. I was nineteen years old, with no property, making a dollar five an hour plucking chickens at the local chicken plant. I could sense that my welcome at home was worn out. It was time for me to move on, but I wasn't sure where to go or how to get there.

At the same time, the world was changing rapidly. Suburbs were springing up all over the country, and America was discovering McDonald's, fast cars, television, and credit cards. A different kind of music by Bill Haley and the Comets and Elvis Presley had replaced those like "Don't Sit under the Apple Tree with Anyone Else but Me." On their way out were the 1950s, which had created a heady atmosphere of good life and prosperity, or so they said. Maybe that was true, but I think it depended on who you were, and where you were.

In the fifties, supposedly, people spent more money because they earned more, but that might have been an illusion. Maybe they spent more because it was easier to borrow and assume more debt.

Also in the fifties, Eisenhower dominated the White House. He was elected the first time because he was a high-ranking general, famed for his leadership in the Normandy invasion that led to the end of the war in Europe. He represented security and trust to Americans weary of the carnage and deprivation of World War II, so no one was really surprised when he was elected for a second term.

Meanwhile, there was a war in Korea that most people didn't really want to think about. I won't say that our country was looking the other way, but Americans were tired of war. Nearly thirty-four thousand Americans died over there, and the total casualty count (military and civilian), was about 2.8 million, counting North Korea, South Korea, China, and the troops of the United Nations. It was called the *forgotten war*, and when it ended in 1954, the American people spent the balance of the decade looking to get ahead.

Though forgotten, the Korean War was not devoid of strife and controversy. If it served no other purpose, the conflict brought Communism with all of its ugliness to public attention. We began to hear stories about captured American soldiers being tortured and forced to make false confessions against their country. Needless to say, these ugly tales were discouraging. They contradicted the way that most Americans chose to view their fighting men.

People like Senator Joe McCarthy took advantage of the situation. McCarthy used his extreme version of patriotism to cast doubt on anyone who dared to disagree with him. Careers were ended, reputations were damaged, and characters were tarnished. McCarthy called his version of things the truth, but he couldn't prove it. Luckily for him, the fear of Communist subversion had become so powerful that he didn't have to prove anything. All he had to do was make sensational accusations; the frenzy of public opinion did the rest.

Beyond all of the fear-mongering and political posturing, Communism was a very real threat. Like the atomic bomb, it was a specter that hung over the heads of everyone in America. Bomb shelters and fallout shelters were created, and school children were drilled in the proper procedures to use in case of nuclear attack. Perhaps subterfuge and disinformation had also been used in World War II, but they were taken to new levels in the late fifties and sixties.

Eventually, however, the steady hand of Eisenhower calmed the nerves of the American public. The man on the street began to breathe a little easier again. After all, we were *here*, and Communism was over *there* somewhere. Eisenhower was able to shut down McCarthy, and most Americans were placated. But the damage wrought by McCarthy's half-truths and misinformation could not be completely undone.

President Eisenhower wanted America and the rest of the world to believe in peaceful coexistence, but that desire did not blind him to reality. He saw the encroachment of Communism in the Pacific Rim as a future threat to Australia, New Zealand, and—eventually—America.

All the while, the average American was barbequing in the backyard, cruising the streets in '57 Chevys, sipping Cherry Cokes, and listening to "Silhouettes on the Shades." All of that might have been good for America, but it certainly wasn't going to stop what was happening in Southeast Asia.

Eisenhower had learned the unpleasant lessons taught by Senator McCarthy. He had seen what the unbridled fear of Communism could do to this country. And maybe that's why he decided to take a secretive approach to attacking the Communist threat. If so, he may have been correct. Secrecy might have been the proper course of action for America at that particular time. I don't know, and I don't think I have the right to judge. I just know it happened: America embarked on a secret war, and the people who fought it were nameless and faceless.

Secrecy works well when everything is going according to plan, but problems with this tactic become obvious when things go wrong. Patriotic soldiers like Francis Gary Powers (who was shot down in a U2 spy plane over Russia) and Allen Pope (who was shot down in a B-26 in Indonesia) were characterized as *mercenaries* and *soldiers of fortune*. Their association with the American military was denied. They were criticized vehemently, and some went so far as to suggest that these brave men should have committed suicide before allowing their country to be embarrassed.

Like many Americans, I tend to believe what I read. I can also be affected physically by the act of reading. I get cold when I read about snow, and I get hungry when I read about food. So when the newspapers proclaimed back then that everything was fine in the world, I had no reason to doubt them. I sincerely believed that everyone everywhere was at peace. Yet somewhere, on the other side of the world, people were fighting for their lives in a place that few Americans had even heard of.

You would think I would have been more cognizant, because I had lived in many places before my parents settled in Noel, Missouri. I was young, of course, but I had experiences that went well beyond typical small-town life. My family had lived on a large Air Force base, where people trained for war daily. I had grown up intermixing with people of varied backgrounds. I was probably equipped to understand world events more than the average small-town kid my age. I just wasn't paying attention.

In those days, Noel had a population of about twelve hundred, and that number is just about the same today. But living in a small town doesn't make you ignorant. The citizens of Noel were uninformed, perhaps, but probably no more so than the rest of the country. America was being sheltered, and most of us liked it. I really don't think it made any difference whether you were raised in the city or on a farm.

Like most small towns, Noel did have its problems, though. The town had limited cultural activities, and jobs for high school graduates were scarce. For most people, escape was the only option.

Dad was raised in McDonald County, where Noel is located. It's probably the poorest county in Missouri, and it was poorer still during the Depression.

Dad joined the army air corps in 1935, and he met my mom in the state of Washington, where I was born at Fort Lewis. A year later, we moved to Spokane, and my brother was born.

Next, Dad was transferred to Clovis, New Mexico, and then Colorado Springs, Colorado, where my sister was born. We traveled a lot, but Dad never forgot that his roots were in Noel. His mother continued to live in a two-room house on Hall Ridge Road, just outside of Noel, and we went there as often as Dad could get leave.

I attended early grade school at Noel, the same school my Dad had attended, and Dorothy Davis was one of my teachers. She was obviously well qualified and later became the school principal, but I remember her as being—for lack of a better word—stern. However, Mom considered *no-nonsense* a more appropriate characterization, and she made it clear that she appreciated Ms. Davis's dedication to her job and to the students she shepherded. Dorothy's maiden name was Rousselot. Her father had been the Noel postmaster at one time. Her brother, Robert, had been raised on Hall Ridge Road too, but I didn't learn anything about him until many years later.

Robert was in his eighties when we actually met at his cattle ranch in Oklahoma. I truly enjoyed his company and that of his lovely wife, Ann. Robert and I talked often, mostly by phone, and I visited him and Ann at their home when I was in the area. He was gruff, but pleasantly so, and he ran his ranch with an iron fist. His boys, one of whom is now a state congressman, called him "Boss."

Robert had graduated from Noel almost twenty years before I had. He had wanted to be a doctor, but the war hindered that idea. Instead, Robert joined the Marines and distinguished himself as a pilot with the Flying Tigers. After the war, he went to work for an airline company in China called Civil Air Transport.

People who knew him later told me that Robert was a "tough man," meaning that he was no-nonsense, like his sister, and professionally dedicated as well. Robert was elevated to vice president of operations for CAT, Inc., the company that purchased 40 percent of Civil Air Transport. Later, in 1959, CAT, Inc. was renamed Air America. Robert left the company in 1963.

Sometime after that, Robert retired to his ranch. Later, when he was inducted into the Oklahoma Aviation Hall of Fame, there was almost no mention of Air America or what it had all been about.

Dad wanted desperately to be in the war, but only about 10 to 20 percent of those in the military actually see combat. The majority are support personnel.

Of course, no fighting man can operate without support personnel, yet saying that to those who wanted to be in action was like saying they were lucky to be playing golf at all, when what they really wanted was to break eighty.

There seems to be a common belief that people who have been in combat are reluctant to talk about their experiences. That's not quite correct. That is, I don't think combat veterans intentionally refuse to discuss it. Rather, the problem is that when you get ready to talk about it, the words to describe the experiences don't readily come to mind. No one wants to come off sounding like they personally did something extraordinary; because the truth is most just did the job they were trained for, but no one wants to belittle the effort either. And while you're groping painfully for the right words, someone invariably says, "Well, he really doesn't want to talk about it." At that point, anything you want to say would sound foolish.

What was there to say anyway? You never really had time to sit around and discuss how you were going to act in a firefight. There was no time for contemplation when you were lifting wounded out of a landing zone under fire. You acted on instinct, derived from hard training, and then it was over almost as fast as it began. Owning a small business when short on capital and knowing your next paycheck would come from the next sale might bring you closer to Jesus than any armed conflict—you've got more time to brood over things, that's for certain.

Also, contrary to popular opinion, I don't think war makes you a better man. You are what you are, and war will not change that. It might show you what kind of man you are, however, and you may not like what you see.

At any rate, somehow, I think Dad knew that Noel was the place for him to fight his battles. He was just looking for his opportunity.

As luck would have it, the Noel postmaster retired, and Mom and Dad campaigned for the position. It was highly contested and understandably so, because the position was appointed by the president in those days, and the appointment was for life. There was no doubt that Dad was qualified. Twenty-five years in a supervisory position with the USAF had prepared him for the task, and he was selected for the appointment. For the first time in more than two decades, he was where he belonged. Now it was time to find where I belonged. At the time, I didn't realize it was going to take almost as long as my Dad.

Several people I knew spent their entire careers at the chicken plant, moving from the line to various supervisory positions. That didn't feel like an option for me. I didn't yet know what I wanted out of life, but it wasn't the chicken plant.

There were other kids my age whose parents owned businesses or farms. They were able to carry on with the family trade. My choices were limited.

I was contemplating all of this on that hot July afternoon in 1960 as I stood in the dirt road that led to my parents' house. The legendary prosperity of the 1950s had not managed to find its way to Noel, Missouri. If it couldn't find its way to me, maybe I'd have to go in search of it myself.

On impulse, I asked for the keys to the car. Without saying where I was going, I drove to Joplin, forty-six miles away. The military recruiting offices were all in one location, and it was lunchtime when I arrived.

All of the recruiters were gone, except for a marine staff sergeant doing some paperwork at his desk. The sign on the wall said, "The Marines Build Men." That sounded good enough for me. I walked on in.

After introducing myself, I asked the sergeant if I could leave for boot camp right away. He told me that I could depart right after the July Fourth holiday.

I had a choice of boot camps, and I decided on San Diego instead of Parris Island. No reason really. I had never been to either, but California sounded warmer.

Mom had tears in her eyes when I told her. Dad was smiling. He'd been there before.

I was inducted on the sixth of July, and I headed to California on my first jet ride with Continental Airlines. This was the first time I had ever done something on my own. I was thrilled and looking forward to the experience.

After that, I came back to Noel for visits, but I never went home again. My home was now somewhere else, and it always would be.

The Making Of A Marine

I started out as a private in the rear ranks. It is difficult to explain why anyone would like boot camp, but the truth is I did enjoy it. I was handy with my fists when the need arose, but I was a skinny kid and I needed some muscle tone. I liked the rigor of learning a trade, albeit fighting, and I quickly put on weight in the right places.

There were some shocks, however.

Foul language had not been allowed in our home, and it wasn't prevalent in my circle of friends at school. So it set me back on my heels the first time I heard a drill instructor utter venomous words and threats that I couldn't begin to contemplate and, quite frankly, seemed humanly impossible, but definitely got my attention.

You had to have experienced boot camp to understand Buddy Hackett's comedy routine included admonition to mothers whose sons were now performing private bathroom duties in public. The commodes in *the head* (what the US Navy and Marine Corps call the bathroom) stood about twenty or so in a row, with no stalls and no toilet seats. When we were instructed to make a "head call" in the morning, twenty guys would sit down at one time and do their business. A person who liked his privacy found it difficult at first, but soon you got used to it.

I discovered that liberals and conservatives were about evenly matched in the corps, and later found bravery in battle had nothing whatsoever to do with political affiliation or belief. Each side would argue heatedly, but when it came to the matter at hand, all of that was forgotten.

I learned quickly that the Marines have their own way of doing things. For example, unless he is on guard duty, a marine does not enter a building while he is covered (wearing a hat). Marines do not salute when uncovered. So, when you see a marine in the movies salute with no cover, you'll know that he is not really a marine and that the director does not know his Marine Corps manners.

My Marine Corps boot camp company. I'm in the third row from the top, eighth from the left.

Along with rewards, there were also disappointments, a statement that is a study about life in general, I suppose. I had never fired a rifle before boot camp. A necessary part of your basic training is getting to know a rifle inside and out, and qualifying at the rifle range. Hours are spent shooting in various positions, which includes standing, prone (lying down), and sitting. The sitting position is normally used for rapid-fire, where you have sixty seconds to go from a standing to a sitting position and to rapidly fire ten rounds at a target two hundred yards away. Ideally, all of the shots are grouped closely inside the center of the target, in the spot typically identified by a red circle called the bull's eye. There are three levels of achievement. Marksman is the lowest level, with sharp shooter being next up, and then expert. I shot at the expert level every day on the range, but on qualification day, my rapid-fire sitting position—which I was good at—grouped just below the bull's eye. I ended up as a sharp shooter on the one day it counted.

I can't say that I was a model soldier, and even back then I had definite ideas about what was right or wrong. A lot of people think it's better to go with the flow, but that's not in my character. Still, I didn't mind tackling any job, but had to work hard to stay up with strenuous physical activity. And I had integrity and knew how to get things done. That might have been why I was made a squad leader.

I took care of the members on my squad, and that included discipline, if necessary. I only weighed a hundred and thirty-five pounds, and there were people in my platoon you wouldn't want to mess with. I didn't pick fights, and tried to avoid them if possible, but if I was against the wall, I didn't back down from anybody.

Maybe the drill instructors saw promise in me as a squad leader or maybe there was some other reason, but eventually they brought me in to be what they called a *house mouse*. My job would be to clean their room, make their beds, and be a "gofer." You know, to "go fer"—or go get—the things they wanted.

Becoming a house mouse would have meant automatic promotion to PFC (private first class) when I graduated from boot camp. Only 10 percent of recruits would make PFC right out of boot camp, so this was a rare opportunity to grab a quick promotion. I should have jumped at the chance, right? But that wasn't exactly what "Marines Build Men" meant to me.

I did not feel honored by the idea of becoming a house mouse. So I looked the DI in the eye, told him that he needed to learn how to make his own bed, and that I hadn't hired on with this outfit to be a chambermaid. I went on to say that I planned on making PFC by what I accomplished in the field with the troops.

The problem is that you don't talk back to a Marine Corps drill instructor. Ever. If you do happen to make that particular mistake, you're in for a painful experience. You also don't look your instructor in the eye. It's called *eyeballing*, and pure trouble comes soon thereafter. I did it anyway. I did, however, request permission to speak.

Everything got quiet, and I could see that the DI was having trouble getting words out. His face was turning red as a beet, and he looked like he was choking.

Finally, he regained his composure and told me in no uncertain words that, as far as he was concerned, I was a private in the rear ranks and that he would personally make sure I stayed that way.

Then came the pain I was telling you about. I spent quite a lot of time in the pushup position, while he ignited pools of lighter fluid under my body. All the while, he was daring me to fall and calling me names that I'd never heard before or since. Let's just say that I got tired of the experience before the drill instructor did.

Contrary to his threats, I still made PFC out of boot camp, which was my goal. One of seven chosen, out of seventy, and I wasn't exactly sure why I had been selected, but I appreciated the promotion doing it my way.

Further, my aptitude test scores showed I qualified for the Marine Aviation Cadet Program, through which, in eighteen months, I could become a pilot and an officer. I hadn't gone for house mouse, but I did jump at the opportunity to fly.

In July of 1961, a year almost to the day after I left home, I was ordered to report to the Chief Naval Aviation Training Command in Pensacola, Florida. I immediately found myself right back in boot camp, with another drill instructor. But this was no ordinary DI. He was bound and determined to make me quit. In fact, that was his job.

It was harder. A lot harder than San Diego had been. For all of the harassment they had given us in San Diego, their goal had been to help us graduate from boot camp. In Pensacola, the goal was to weed out anyone who couldn't handle the strain. They *wanted* us to quit, and they did their level best to make it happen. Quitting (or failing) meant immediate removal from the program, and it was back to the rank of PFC.

The military discipline there was at least as strict as boot camp had been, and the physical endurance training was nothing short of grueling. But, as difficult as those challenges were, they were not the hardest part. The hard part was ground school.

They crammed our heads with aerodynamics, navigation, leadership, history, and a whole range of other subjects. The curriculum was difficult, and I frankly was not prepared for the amount of studying that was required.

I thought I could easily handle the military discipline, but infractions were numerous and—to a certain extent—frivolous. I often found myself on the parade field that was commonly called *the grinder*, marching with my rifle.

I had thought I was pretty smart, but I learned that being smart and being knowledgeable are two completely different things. I struggled to keep up with ground school, and it didn't help that many of my classmates were college graduates.

Somehow, though, I got through it. I was nowhere near the top of my class, but I did finish. I had worked hard to finish, as I had always thought I could excel at any endeavor I worked hard at. Perhaps that alone should have made me happy, but it didn't. I had not excelled so I was disappointed. I watched the guys at the top of my class and knew they had earned their positions, and that was a bitter pill to swallow.

Looking back, I think I got through preflight on guts alone. It damn sure wasn't through superior ability.

Finding myself measured and wanting was not something I could be proud of. I was highly apprehensive about continuing in the aviation program, and I hadn't even seen an airplane yet. But I refused to quit.

Learning to Fly

We now were officially cadets, with the same rank as a chief warrant officer, which included officer club privileges and better pay. I bought a 1957 Pontiac to get around in and started getting ready for flight instruction.

Primary was taught in a Beechcraft T-34 Mentor. It was a pretty good aircraft, with a single engine and good performance. Flying came relatively easy for me. Perhaps it was because that's what I wanted to do.

Even acrobatics came easily, but initially I had trouble with airsickness when doing the maneuvers. I upchucked often, and kept three barf bags in my flight suit, but kept on going. My instructor told me he wouldn't release me to go solo if I couldn't control it.

Over time, I found that some things didn't sit well in my stomach before flying, so I avoided eating them on the morning of my check flight. I left my barf bags on the ground. If I upchucked during my check flight, I knew I wouldn't be allowed to fly anymore, so there was no point in taking them. It turned out I didn't need them anyway. I flew a perfect check flight.

I first soloed on a clear, crisp day. I did all of the maneuvers: stalls (powering on and off), spins, loops, barrel rolls, and full Cuban eights.

I think I could have stayed up all day, fuel permitting. When you're up in the air by yourself, the sound of the engine fades, there is a hush, like being in church with no one present but you. The airplane and you are one and the same. It's like you spread your own wings and glide with the wind.

Barrel rolls were my favorite acrobatic maneuver, and I did them as often as I could. A barrel roll is a smooth, balanced maneuver. On the day of my check flight, I looked to my left, or right side, spotted a lake, or some other landmark, and picked up some speed. I started a loop by smoothly pulling the nose up and turning so that I was upside down and 90 degrees from my original heading. I looked up and back, and saw the landmark in front of my nose. I kept pulling smoothly, and turning, until I ended up right where I had started.

I was a lot better in the cockpit than I was in the classroom. My flight grades were excellent, but my ground-school grades were mediocre at best. After graduation, I wanted to get into the jet pipeline, flying T2 Buckeyes in Meridian, Mississippi. Things didn't work out that way. Instead, I was sent to fly T-28s at Whiting Field in Milton, Florida. Another disappointment. I still had another chance for jets, however, if I excelled in the T-28. I was determined to do just that.

Allen Cates in 1962 with the T-28 Trainer.

I liked the T-28. It was a single-engine trainer, with a nine-cylinder radial engine and 1,425 horsepower at sea level. It was far more powerful than the Beechcraft.

We started with basic flying, and then went onto soloing, full acrobatics, formation flying, and gunnery. Takeoffs were a hoot, as the T-28 would pin your ears back at full throttle.

It is hard to describe flying. You don't really operate aircraft. You wrap it around yourself, and you became part of the structure. You don't horse the aircraft around, or jam the controls, and you don't think about the movements required to stay in balanced flight. You feel it inside yourself, and you automatically add appropriate control movements when required.

You also don't turn an aircraft. You rotate yourself on an axis, and the airplane goes with you. The aircraft does not control you; you control the aircraft. You're not just along for the ride. Power controls altitude, and nose position controls air speed. You and the aircraft move as a single unit, and you learn to control pitch, yaw, and roll precisely and in balance.

We used 50-caliber machine guns mounted under the T-28 wing for gunnery training, and I loved it. The instructor towed a target attached to his aircraft with a cable that extended well to the rear. The student was in a position above and off to the side of the target. The procedure was to roll into a turn, while maintaining balanced flight with the rudders, and descend so that the target passed in front of your nose. It was necessary to lead the target and start firing when you felt you were in a position where the bullets would meet the target. When clear of the target, you used the excess speed attained while diving to carry you back up above the target on the opposite side. This training was more of an experience rather than a lesson in becoming proficient at air-to-air gunnery, but it was great fun and ended way too quickly.

Next, we moved on to carrier qualifications. Landing on an aircraft carrier is a flying activity reserved for U.S. Navy and Marine Corps pilots, and it is a source of pride to master it. Navy and Marine Corps aircraft are equipped with tail hooks, sometimes referred to as arresting hooks that are lowered by the pilot when landing on a carrier. The carrier has a series of cables stretched across the landing area. These cables originally were on pulleys and attached to sand bags, but today's aircraft are much heavier and require far more sophistication. The flight procedure requires a precision landing allowing the tail hook to engage the cable. The cable is stretched and the kinetic energy of the landing aircraft is transferred mechanically through the cable and finally hydraulically to an arresting engine located below the flight deck.

Older carriers had straight decks making it impossible to touch down and immediately take off if the aircraft tail hook failed to catch a cable. Should the aircraft fail to catch a cable the landing gear would be caught by a three-to-four foot high net known as the *barrier*. If the aircraft caught a cable upon touchdown, the barrier could be quickly lowered to allow aircraft to taxi over it. The final safety net was the *barricade*, a large, fifteen-foot high net that prevented landing aircraft from crashing into other aircraft parked on the bow. Aircraft carriers are now designed with angled decks, which are much safer because if you miss the cables you can add power and continue straight ahead with nothing in your way.

The approach to landing must be on a precise angle that allows the aircraft to arrive and touch down exactly on target. At one time, a Landing Signal Officer (LSO) controlled the approach angle. He was a specially trained naval aviator using colored paddles that could be seen by the landing aircraft. They were lighted at night. A paddle was held in each hand and the position of the paddles provided clues to the pilot whether he was too low or too high and allowed him to adjust accordingly. At the exact moment the LSO gave a signal to cut power allowing the aircraft to drop smartly on to the deck and catch the cable with the tail hook dangling below and to the rear of the aircraft. Later, the paddles were replaced with an optical lens with a ball in the center commonly called a "meatball." A row of green datum lights sits horizontal and the meatball is on a vertical scale that provides the aircraft's relative position to the proper glide slope. A low ball means you are too low and a high ball means you are too high. The ball changes to a red color if you're too low. Flashing red lights controlled manually by the LSO light up if he determines your approach is not safe for landing and is a mandatory requirement to add power and climb back up for another approach.

We practiced over and over again at an outlying field until we learned to plant the bird right on the numbers of our simulated carrier deck with absolute precision. Of course, our deck wasn't moving, and we practiced in daylight with good weather. Landing on the pitching deck of an aircraft carrier at night in heavy weather would probably be a horse of a different color. But we still felt like we had accomplished something.

Finally, the day came to do it on the real thing. The USS *Antietam* had served with honor in Korea, and now she was being used as a training carrier in the Gulf of Mexico. She had an angled deck so that she could launch and recover at the same time.

To qualify for carriers, we had to perform two "touch and go" landings and four arrested landings, in which the tail hook caught a cable that rapidly slowed the aircraft to a stop. What an absolute thrill! An arrested landing feels like an elevator coming to a stop. Each time we did one, we were spotted and signaled to go to full power with the brakes on, and then—with a wave—we accelerated off the deck out over the water, with the canopy open in case we had to ditch. I'll never forget the sound of the wind, the roar of the engine, and my body full of adrenaline. No one could hear me screaming out the Marine Corp hymn and a few *ye-haws!* as I pulled up my landing gear and circled around for another pass.

Like gunnery training, it was over way too quickly. Heading back in, I threw my single-bar marine cadet wings out of the cockpit, and into the slipstream of the aircraft. I was carrier-qualified now, entitled to wear the double-bar wings reserved for pilots who had accomplished the feat.

I was elated and ready to head to Corpus Christi, Texas, for F9 and F11 jet training. That was where I belonged.

But another disappointment loomed. For a couple of days it looked like I would be assigned to the jet training program, but instead I was sent to the helicopter program.

My alternatives narrowed rapidly. I could go for instrument training in the SNB (the Navy term for the C-45) and then on to fly helicopters. Or I could drop on-request and go back to being a PFC with the ground Marines.

My classmate Doyle Baker threatened to do just that and meant it. He had spent more than a year with one thing on his mind: he was going to fly an F4 Phantom jet, and, by God, was *not* going to fly a helicopter.

At the other end of the scale was Bill Martin, who excelled in everything: military, physical fitness, and flying. He was at the top of the class, so he was automatically selected for jets. But Bill loved helicopters. That's what he had come into the program for. Like Doyle, he threatened to drop out of the aviation program if he couldn't get what he wanted. Of course, there was one difference in Bill's case—he had already been a commissioned officer when he came to flight school, and they couldn't take that away from him.

By this time, the Navy had spent several hundred thousand dollars training both of them, so sending them back to the ground corps would be a complete waste. It was a no-brainer; they swapped. Bill went on to helicopters, and Doyle got to fly jets.

Later, Bill served with me in Vietnam, and he was as happy as a clam to be flying helicopters. In turn, I guess Doyle became a pretty good F4 pilot. I heard that he shot down a MIG in North Vietnam.

Bill went to work for Bell Helicopter after he separated from the Marine Corps, and he assisted with developing the Osprey, a tilt-rotor aircraft that could land like a helicopter and fly like an airplane, before he finally retired in Dallas-Ft. Worth.

They were both good pilots, and they had both gotten what they wanted—what they had worked for. I hadn't. I was in a funk. I'm sure everybody had worked as hard as I had, but this was the worst disappointment I had ever experienced.

I actually thought about giving up flying. It was a bitter, bitter letdown. It wasn't in me to quit though, so, very reluctantly, I reported for duty and instruction in the SNB. Needless to say, I was not happy. The SNB was a fine aircraft, but it wasn't a jet.

We flew in teams, and my partner was a large, redheaded, good-natured man named Corcoran. Naturally, Corky was his nickname. Corky was a fine person and a good-looking kid. Women fell all over him without him saying a word.

Up to this stage, I had been schooled in flying while maintaining visual contact with the ground. However, you can't always see the ground and in clouds you must rely on instruments in the cockpit to maintain altitude and level flight. You must also learn to descend through clouds and fly a specific approach pattern designed for each particular airport all over the world. Each airport has published approach patterns that are depicted in printed templates that are in a bound ring binder. These approach plates are continually upgraded and it is the pilot's responsibility to maintain them and keep them up to date. The approach plates include the frequency of the navigation aids, and radio frequencies for communications to the tower and approach control at each airport. They include the proper altitudes for each segment of the approach that allows a pilot to arrive at his destination blind, descend to and align the aircraft with the appropriate runway and once below the clouds land the aircraft safely. Flying on instruments means flying without visual reference to the ground using the gages in the cockpit and requires intensive training.

By this time, I had polished my academic skills pretty well. I knew how to study and how to pass tests, so Corky and I blazed through the course in short order. Knowing the jargon probably made it easier, however, so had I been more familiar with the lingo and the literature earlier on, I would have done much better and gotten the jet slot I wanted.

Regardless, I was to go onto helicopters, and Corky, who was a cadet in the Navy, would finish training in the S2F, a twin-engine antisubmarine aircraft. And then, the unexpected happened. Corky quit. Just like that. He had always seemed mature and levelheaded, and I tried to reason with him. But he had made up his mind. He did not want to be an officer.

The Navy acted like Corky had stiffed them, and I guess he had. But I always felt like something else must have happened to cause him to make the decision he did. I have no idea what changed Cork's mind, and I'm sure that I'll never know. All I know is that his decision didn't make any sense to me.

The last time I saw Corky, he was in an enlisted sailor's uniform on a work detail. I shook my head and went on to helicopter training.

I had adapted to airplanes immediately, but flying the bubble-canopy Bell G-47 helicopter was like standing on a basketball with one leg and with your eyes closed. Yet, this was my station in life, and I was determined to play the cards that had been dealt to me.

With a fighter pilot's heart, I learned to hover, go up and down, and land with no engine (a technique called *autorotation*). In a strong wind, you would fly the G-47 forward but actually travel backward. This did not add to my appreciation of the aircraft. I should add that fifty years later, the G-47 Bell became a very popular aircraft and quite expensive to own. But at the time, for a young man who wanted to fly swept-wing jets, it was difficult to be excited about this machine that appeared to have a lot of parts all going in different directions at the same time. A lot of people loved the helicopter, however, so my attitude about it did not sit well with some of them. I finally decided to handle my task as best I could and accept what I couldn't change.

Allen Cates receiving his wings and helicopter certification December 1962

After completing the G-47 curriculum, I moved on to the H-19, which had a seven-cylinder radial engine and was much bigger than the Bell. Despite its size, the H-19 was underpowered. We used to say that, in the mountains, the H-19 would hardly carry verbal messages. It had been a real workhorse in Korea though, and it had saved a lot of lives by transporting wounded soldiers to aid stations faster than they could travel by ground.

We were fitted in uniforms that took me a year to pay for, and—just for the hell of it—I purchased a Marine Corps sword that still hangs on a wall in my office. We graduated as naval aviators and were designated as naval helicopter pilots. I received my wings and my gold bars as a brand new second lieutenant.

It shouldn't have been anticlimactic, but it was. At twenty-one, I had been in the Corps two and a half years, and I felt like an old man who had faced too many disappointments. I saw myself as seasoned and world-weary. I was wrong, of course.

Squadron Training And Preparing For War

The training command doesn't actually teach you to be a helicopter pilot. You learn the basics, but advanced training for combat conditions is accomplished when you get to your squadron. So I was ordered to Marine Corps Air Station Santa Ana, in Tustin, California. The Air Station had been established in 1942 as Naval Air Station Santa Ana, a base for airship operations in support of the United States Navy's coastal patrol efforts during WWII. NAS Santa Ana was then decommissioned in 1949.

In 1951, the facility was reactivated as Marine Corps Air Station Santa Ana, to support the Korean War. It was the country's first air facility developed solely for helicopter operations. It was renamed Marine Corps Air Station Tustin in 1970.

In 1963, the Marines had two primary helicopters: the H-37 (commonly called the Deuce), and the UH34D. Sikorsky Aircraft manufactured both.

The Deuce was an enormous aircraft, powered by two R-2800 engines with eighteen cylinders each, in two rows of nine. The H-34 was a single-engine helicopter with one row of nine cylinders. I never flew the Deuce, but of the two, it was reportedly the better aircraft. It was certainly preferred by the Marine Corps.

Sikorsky UH-34D. Photo used by permission of Tom Lum.

The Deuce was capable of carrying a huge load for a helicopter, close to 5,000 pounds, and it was much faster than the H-34. The Deuce had also held the world's speed record for several years, at 162 miles per hour. Loading was accomplished from the front of the helicopter, through two large clamshell doors that were big enough to drive a jeep through.

The H-34 was meant to be an interim aircraft while the Deuce was being manufactured, because Sikorsky couldn't build the Deuce quickly enough to satisfy the demand. Eventually, however, the H-34 became the primary aircraft, until replaced with the tandem rotor H-46 in the late sixties.

The main difference between a fixed-wing aircraft and a helicopter is stability. In many respects, the theory of flight is similar: altitude is controlled with power and airspeed is controlled with nose position above or below the horizon commonly called "nose attitude." In the cockpit in level flight the nose of the aircraft will be observed at a specific place on the horizon and usually just below the horizon. Raising the nose above this position dissipates airspeed and lowering below this position increases airspeed. The best performance is obtained when you wrap the aircraft around yourself, making a single unit. But, where this was easy for me in a fixed-wing, it was exceedingly difficult in a helicopter.

When you trim up a fixed-wing aircraft in level flight and release the controls, it will stay in position. Even if you pull up, push down, or roll left or right, the aircraft will tend to return to its original position. A helicopter has no natural tendency for stable flight. In a helicopter, if you release the controls, the aircraft immediately becomes unstable. If you continue to keep your hands off the controls, it will quickly crash.

If you move a control in an airplane, you don't have to adjust any other controls, except the rudders to keep the ball in the center—or, in other words, to stay in balanced flight without skidding. In a helicopter, if you adjust one control, you have to make compensating changes in all of the other controls. It's a bit like trying to stand on an object shaped like an egg. To keep from falling, you must be constantly alert and continually balanced. If one part of your body moves, even slightly, you have to move other parts at the same time. If you can't manage this unceasing balancing act, you fall.

In a light helicopter, for example a G-47 bubble-canopy Bell, the control pressures are light enough to be mechanically linked. You can get a sense of how the aircraft is performing by the way the controls feel in your hands. In a larger helicopter, even the H-34, you can never move the controls without hydraulic assistance. Unfortunately, this hydraulic assistance isolates you from any sense of control. The controls give you no clues about the performance of the aircraft.

Mastering the H-34 took time. Just about when you thought you had it nailed, the helicopter would quickly show you the error of your ways. A 1,525-horsepower hotrod engine that breathed fire and brimstone powered it. The skin of the aircraft was made of magnesium, which is lighter than aluminum, but creates oxygen when it burns, making it practically impossible to extinguish. If an H-34 caught on fire, there was virtually no way to stop the damned thing from burning.

My good friend, the late David Kendall, once told me in his Tennessee drawl, "Allen, if you parked a brand new American LaFrance fire engine next to an H-34 on fire, what would happen is you would lose a helicopter and a damn good fire engine."

Many flight crewmembers were seriously injured or killed due to fire-related injuries after crashing in an H-34.

I looked at the H-34 when I arrived in Santa Ana and realized that it was my penance for mediocre ground-school performance in flight school. As I had brought this condition upon myself, then, slashing my wrists or wearing sackcloth and ashes didn't seem to be acceptable responses. It was better, I realized, to accept my fate and strive to do better. The H-34 and I were going to learn to be friends, one way or another.

After WWII, Marine first lieutenant pilots who did not have college educations were offered the choice of accepting reduction to the rank of master sergeant, or separation from the Corps. Enlisted naval aviation pilots (NAP) had been in the Navy and Marine Corps since 1916 and it was considered an honored profession, but going from officer to enlisted was akin to a slap in the face. Not because master sergeant wasn't honorable, but because it was a demotion without cause or infraction. It was a tough choice, but many accepted it rather than separation.

Later, the Marine Corps provided another option, because the flying sergeant program was to be eliminated. The new choices were to accept the chief warrant officer position, which was supposed to be a specialty position, or that of second lieutenant, which was somewhat demeaning, because they had already been first lieutenants several years before. Most chose warrant officer, but some became second lieutenants, which, as it turned out, was the wiser choice. The second lieutenants were quickly promoted to first lieutenants, and then to captains and higher. The warrant officers, on the other hand, remained warrants, and—instead of specialists—were considered lower in rank than shave tail second lieutenants.

This led to a lot of resentment, but the warrants were some of the finest pilots the Marines ever had, and they were great flight instructors. I learned a great deal from them, and no one, to my knowledge, looked upon them as subordinates, but instead as mentors.

When I first arrived on station I was assigned to Marine Medium Helicopter Squadron 363 (HMM-363) for about six months. I made helicopter aircraft commander (HAC) fairly quickly, and I volunteered for every flight-instruction job available. We were encouraged to fly cross-country on the weekends to any place we wanted as long as we landed at an approved landing facility, and filed a flight plan letting the squadron know where we were going. I often took advantage of this privilege. I went north to San Francisco, south to San Diego and 29 Palms, west to Catalina Island, and east to the Luke and

Davis-Monthan Air Force bases. I was instructed in hot weather training in 29 Palms California, landing on small zones in the mountains called pinnacle landing zones, and cold weather training in the snow near Reno, Nevada. Soon thereafter, I was made an instructor pilot for new officers.

The squadron's logistics officer, Captain George Boemerman, who later would be transferred to HMM-365 with me, had been sent to logistics school and wasn't available for an upcoming scheduled training exercise. For some reason, I was given the job of handling logistics for a training exercise aboard ship, which included deployment to a tent city at Camp Pendleton, California. My job was to coordinate the departure of personnel from the ship and to have the tent city erected and in place when they arrived. This was the first time I had ever handled logistics work, and the sheer volume of equipment was astonishing to me. The tent pegs alone required six large trucks.

Lieutenant Lockner, who was not an aviator, was handling the material movements on land, and I was handling personnel movements aboard ship. There was no way to communicate with Lockner while he was ashore, but we had gone over the requirements together prior to deployment.

Lockner had roomed just across the hall from me at Santa Ana, and he had introduced me to chess. He was an intellectual and would read a book while we played. The distraction didn't keep him from beating me every game. He was certainly smart enough to handle the logistics job, but I didn't know whether he could work under such pressure. He had certainly never experienced any pressure from my chess playing.

The night of the deployment from ship to land the sky was filled with clouds and rain was falling heavily making flight operations difficult and the activity was hectic. I had everybody assigned to a specific aircraft, and it should have run like clockwork, but when things kicked off, the aircraft were not in sequence. People would rush to a helicopter, and, in the rain, I had no idea who was getting on which aircraft. My carefully prepared manifests were flying in the wind.

If a crash occurred, how would anyone know who was on board, who had survived, and who hadn't?

I knew who was still aboard the ship, so I figured I could line everybody up and find out who was missing. This was not how it was supposed to have happened, but I needed to do something.

I tried to instill my plan, but Marine Corps captains scrambling to find space aboard the helicopters don't pay much attention to brand new second lieutenants. On top of that, a marine captain who was part of the ship's company and probably didn't like it seemed to be delighted to harass me in front of everybody while all hell was breaking loose. He wouldn't come down and do it personally but used the squawk box so that everyone could hear.

I finally told him over the radio, "Look, Mister, I'm doing the best I can, and if you know how to do it better, then come down here and give me a hand."

That didn't go over very well, until a friendly senior captain, whose name I never knew came over and told me, "Al, just have everyone write his name on a piece of paper and hand it to you as he goes out to the aircraft. When you fill the helicopter up, staple the stack of papers together, and write down the number of the aircraft."

It worked, and I was grateful. He was a professional in every way and did not need to prove his authority by demeaning his subordinates. He assisted when the need was apparent without seeking favor. That kind of person I would follow anywhere.

I left the ship on the last helicopter, but now I had a new worry. What if Lockner hadn't managed to get the tent city erected? There were going to be some highly pissed-off, tired, and wet Marines waiting for me on the beach, sure as hell.

When we landed in the dark, I was afraid to even get out of the helicopter. But, sure enough, Lockner had come through. Cooking fires were going, people were laughing, and if I could have found Lockner, I would have hugged him, although that wouldn't go over too well in a Marine Corps tent city.

I was slapped on the back good-naturedly, and some well-meaning person handed me a glass of whisky. I took one drink and collapsed on a bunk without waking until morning.

All of this was part of the experience I needed before moving up the ladder.

Later, I was transferred to HMM-365, commanded by Lieutenant Colonel

Joe Koler. HMM-365 was an expeditionary force, and was designated to rotate to Okinawa in the fall of 1964, and then go on to a place called Vietnam that most of us had little knowledge of.

You had to volunteer to be in the squadron. We received quite a bit of training aboard ship, including night landings on a helicopter carrier, which was similar to the old straight-deck carriers from Korea and WWII.

My executive officer for HMM-365 was a major and a former flying sergeant. He fought in three wars: World War II, Korea, and Vietnam. Warren Gustafson was an excellent pilot and a fine person. He was tough on new second lieutenants, but he was fair, and I could accept fair. Gus, as he was affectionately called when he retired from the service, later went to work for Air America, a company I knew nothing about at the time.

Just before transferring to HMM-365, I was asked if I wanted to volunteer for T-28 duty in someplace in Southeast Asia called Laos. At that time I knew nothing about Laos either, but getting out of helicopters and flying a high-performance *anything* electrified me, so I responded with, "Sir, yes, sir!" I was ready to leave at that very moment but never heard any more about that strange offer. Eventually, I realized it wasn't going to happen, and later I found out why. Air America had plenty of experienced pilots to fly T-28s. They weren't about to allow an outside person to come in to steal their thunder. I also didn't know at the time that the 1962 Geneva Accords forbade active military pilots to operate in Laos. Of course, I could have immediately been removed from service and placed with Air America as a civilian, but I wasn't quite ready for that. I needed some experience under my belt.

Vietnam

In the early fall of 1964, the squadron deployed to Okinawa. George Boemerman handled the logistics, along with his subordinate, Lieutenant Dietrich Koletty. Judging from my experience while with HMM-363, it was a monumental job, and they accomplished it masterfully.

The U.S. Navy made photoreconnaissance flights over Laos in 1964. They were pretty sure North Vietnam was infiltrating the south through Laos and needed documented proof to confront the North Vietnamese government. The photo-recon birds were unarmed and did not use armed escorts either. Such an act would have been a direct violation of the Geneva Accords, and every administration from Eisenhower to Nixon desperately wanted to be seen as honorable to the general public.

In the summer of 1964, Lieutenant Chuck Klusman, flying an RF8 Crusader was shot down and captured. The Navy wanted to go in and get their man out, but the State Department was afraid that a military rescue attempt might cause an international incident; they preferred to keep things quiet.

Air America tried to get Lieutenant Klusman out but encountered intense ground fire. One Air America crewmember was wounded, and—with the absence of air cover—the pickup was almost impossible.

There was ample criticism, and the Air America crews were unjustly accused of dillydallying and being reluctant to go in harm's way. Air America's downed flight crews did not have anyone to speak on their behalf, but the

Navy's hierarchy was adamant. They *would* have armed escort and their flight crews *would* be rescued. As it turned out, Klusman had escaped by his own ingenuity, and showed up one day in an outlying field, where he was safely transported to Thailand. A few days after the shoot-down the Navy's photo-recon aircraft had armed escorts, and once again one aircraft was shot down, but this time Air America made the rescue.

The Gulf of Tonkin incident *supposedly* occurred in August of 1964, and this may have triggered an increased American military presence in Vietnam. Regardless of the reason and justification, real or surreal, we were going to Vietnam, and we were going to war.

HMM-365 did not go directly to Vietnam or stay there for the entire year.[1] In our first period there, from about October until around January of 1965, we acted in direct support to the army of South Vietnam. We also conducted training for the Vietnamese helicopter pilots, with the idea that we would be turning the war over to them in the near future. It didn't work out that way, and we came back in May 1965.

Now, we were supporting the United States Marines. Instead of living in the old French quarters with maid service and an in-house bar, we now dwelled in tents next to the runway.

I sincerely believe that Joe Koler helped save my life in Vietnam, and again later in Laos, with a single statement that I never forgot. Some of the pilots had complained they had busted a gut to rescue a wounded marine, only to find men who had minor injuries or were simply ill. I didn't complain, but I knew what they meant. Colonel Koler said that the degree of the emergency was not a factor, and that every airlift mission should be conducted safely, with no thought whatsoever about the condition of the person to be evacuated.

His words hit home. I realized that, sooner or later, I had to land and be exposed to enemy fire. If I came in too hot, or departed without first determining that I could get out safely, I could end up burning on the rocks—and killing myself and wrecking my aircraft wouldn't help the evacuee in the slightest.

I actually think I was able to accomplish more by using that attitude, and,

1 Enrique B. del Rosario best describes the history of HMM-365 on his website at: http://www.angelfire.com/de/HMM365Vietnam.

after that, I rarely turned down a mission. Rather, I found a way to accomplish each difficult mission in a unique manner, without injuring the crew or the evacuee, or damaging the aircraft. I'm not saying that we didn't have injuries and deaths, but compared to other squadrons, our casualties were relatively low and I attribute that to Joe Koler's leadership.

Lieutenant Colonel Koler was awarded the Legion of Merit before our tour was completed, and I feel he deserved it. The unit he commanded received the Presidential Unit Citation and the Navy Unit Citation. I believe that he was promoted to general because he had what it took to be a flag officer and was recognized accordingly.

I found out something about myself in Vietnam. Flying the H-34 Stinger (described on del Rosario's website http://www.angelfire.com/de/HMM365Vietnam) was the closest I ever got to being a fighter pilot, though the comparison is difficult to imagine. The H-34 was a poorly designed concept. Its rockets were made for jet aircraft and would not fly straight and true, unless they were fired at airspeeds of at least 275 knots, which is far faster than any helicopter. When you fired them from an H-34, they would fly off in all directions, because all the fins wouldn't open. The gun sight was a fixed sight, and you had to point the aircraft at the target to line up the guns, because the rocket pods and guns were fixed as well as you can see in the picture of a H-34 gun ship.

H-34 Gun Ship

Photo taken from http://www.angelfire.com/de/HMM365Vietnam/, permission of del Rosario.

Unfortunately, neither the H-34 nor any other helicopter was made to point, although later helicopter designers got smart enough to aim the guns, instead of trying to point the entire aircraft.

Fully loaded with armor plating, guns, rockets, machine-gun crew, and fuel, you had to roll the aircraft off to get airborne. On a gun run, the heavily loaded aircraft wanted to keep on going through the pull-out. If you weren't careful, the inertia could smash you into the ground.

Our job was to kill people. I understood the reasoning and the necessity, but it wasn't something I was really proud of afterward. I could not take comfort from the experience, except when I was protecting another aircraft or personnel on the ground, and even then it left me with a sense of remorse.

Medical evacuation was different. Saving another person's life gave me a euphoric feeling that really is indescribable. I would like to believe that I saved lives over there by extracting wounded soldiers quickly and getting them safely to aid stations. I am glad I was a part of that activity.

I suspect there was some level of addiction to the adrenaline rush I received when pitting myself against the enemy. Yet there was something about the war in Vietnam that bothered me. I did a lot of reading prior to deployment. Eugene Burdick and William J. Lederer's novel *The Ugly American*, and *Hell in a Very Small Place* by Bernard B. Fall are two of the books that spring to mind. Reading these books should have provided valuable lessons on how not to conduct a war in Vietnam. Yet seeing it first hand, I felt like we were making the same mistakes these books described and that the French had made many years earlier.

I detested Communism, which I felt, and still feel, is a cruel hoax that oppressed masses of unsuspecting people so that a very few can live the good life. Yet I wasn't sure whether the North Vietnamese were truly Communist or if they just wanted to control their own country. On the other hand, their method of achieving their goal, whatever it was, included murder, rape, and pillaging.

The South Vietnamese government had serious problems too and corruption was one of them. But really, all they wanted was to be left alone. Yet, had America not intervened, would we have experienced the peace that has been enjoyed along the Pacific Rim for the past thirty years?

However, I still have problems understanding the rationale for what I observed. I had never been to war before, but to me, this seemed like a strange way of going about it. General Victor Krulak, a Marine Corps hero, came to Da Nang, gathered us together, and told us that there was a lot of war ahead and that we shouldn't be in too much of a hurry. He went on to say that we could not carry loaded guns, and that we must have permission from higher authority to actively engage the enemy. I guess you could say that I liked the work, but I didn't think much of the war and passive restraint was a difficult concept to grasp.

Secretary of Defense Robert McNamara came over and declared that we would soon defeat the enemy by making the seventeenth parallel impenetrable with barbed war, mines, and even motion detectors.

Supposedly, after the job was done, he asked a junior enlisted man working a bulldozer within the DMZ (Demilitarized Zone) if he thought the seventeenth parallel was impenetrable. The junior man agreed that it was.

McNamara then asked him, "Don't you agree this will quickly end the war?"

The reply was, "Uh, no, sir. I don't believe so."

Surprised and agitated, McNamara asked, "Why not?"

"Uh, well, sir … the North Vietnamese don't *come* this way."

That was true. The Ho Chi Minh Trail, stretching from North Vietnam to the delta in South Vietnam, ran along the Vietnamese/Laos border bypassing the DMZ. The trail would soon become a barb in America's side, and it would remain one of our biggest problems for the rest of the war. It was destined to be the road that led our enemies to Saigon and ended the war ten years later.

Vietnam was a country filled with ethnic minorities, many of whom had filtered down from China across the Red River. Over the years, the people in the southern regions of Vietnam had intermarried with Cambodians. Vietnamese in the north did not have this outside genetic influence. Over time, they became generally taller than their countrymen to the south and had lighter complexions.

The French had been in Vietnam for many years too and had exercised great influence. French Indo-China was formed in 1887 and included what is now known as Vietnam and the kingdom of Cambodia. Laos was included a few years later. The federation lasted until 1954. The separation of South and North Vietnam occurred after the Vietminh defeated the French. Free elections were supposed to be held then, but it was obvious to the leaders of the newly formed South Vietnam that they would lose to candidates from the north.

The truly indigenous people of Vietnam are the *Montagnards,* who dwell along the central highlands. They were fierce fighters, hunting tigers with spears, but were afraid of ghosts. The American Army, especially the Special Forces, trained them to fight.

The first time I saw Montagnards, they were dressed in starched uniforms with red scarves, and they all carried automatic weapons. They were hard-core and afraid of no man. Our job that day was to carry them into battle against a garrison of North Vietnam soldiers located just south of Da Nang. I vividly remember seeing them with their heads held high, anxious to get down to it.

When you're conducting the preflight inspection routine on an H-34, you have to open the clamshell doors to inspect the engine and check for leaks. One of the Montagnard soldiers was leaning against the helicopter when Chuck Swan, a larger-than-average man and an aircraft commander, completed the inspection and closed the doors with a bang. Chuck felt a tap on his arm and looked down to see the soldier calmly pointing to his hand, which was caught in the door. Chuck hurriedly released the door, knowing he had inadvertently caused a serious injury. The soldier walked off shaking his hand as if nothing had happened.

Holy crap! I thought. *These guys are tougher than nails. The North Vietnamese troops don't have a chance.*

We were supposed to pick those Montagnards up after the battle was over, but we didn't, because there were no survivors left to pick up. Every single one of them had been killed.

I'm sure they killed many more of the enemy before they succumbed, but two things were becoming apparent to me. One was the need to respect the enemy. He was not a monkey in a tree, as some people believed. Second, North Vietnam was willing to sacrifice hundreds of thousands to achieve their goal, and they would not be hindered by pomp and circumstance.

Much of my time in Vietnam was spent flying soldiers into battle, backing off to a safe area to await their fate, and then going back in to retrieve them. Often, they were seriously wounded or dead. There was no real safe area, per se.

Sometimes, the enemy turned out to be a woman—or even a child—who sympathized with the North, or was forced to act on their behalf.

Yet life went on for most of the South Vietnamese, as if the war was something they were not concerned with, as long as it did not directly affect them. No matter where we went, while waiting to make an infiltration or exfiltration, a small girl or boy would show up out of nowhere with a bucket of iced-down soda for sale.

The Vietnamese traditional dress, called the *Áo Dài,* is one of the most elegant and beautiful dresses for women. It's very simple, consisting of a close-fitting blouse, with long panels in the front and back, which fall loosely over white trousers. We would be sitting there waiting to go into battle, and a group of these ladies would come riding by on their bicycles, wearing these tantalizing dresses and conical hats. They paid no attention to us whatsoever and acted as if they were in the safest place possible.

Old women would come by with carts filled with small, freshly baked loaves of bread that were occasionally filled with spiced meat. They were absolutely delicious. This was not war as I had imagined it.

The Marine Corps birthday is a time-honored tradition celebrated by Marines on November 10 of every year, wherever they happen to be. A cake is usually served, and cut by the oldest and the youngest marine present. For HMM-365 on this particular day, the honor went to Gunnery Sergeant Michael Caruselle and Private Angel Torres. This was the first war for Torres, who was still in his teens, and the third for "Gunny" Caruselle, who first enlisted in the Marines prior to World War II.

A little fun was needed anyway. The torrential rain pour had been going on for days, and spirits were dampened, as it was difficult to find a dry place anywhere. It was far worse for the indigenous Vietnamese, however, as flooding was severe enough to create a life or death situation for many. Therefore, HMM-365 was asked to assist.

When it comes to assisting, there is no one better to ask than the Marines. There was no hesitation, and we quickly went to the flight line, loaded up, and headed south where most of the flooding was. We didn't have to go far. There was very little land in sight. People were on top of houses, waving at us and begging for help. The enemy was there too creating a strange situation for us: one group was in dire need of rescue and another group was trying to shoot us down.

We discovered afterward that we had rescued friend and foe alike. That was pretty much inevitable. There was no way to know the difference, and we'd had to put all such questions out of our mind while concentrating on the task at hand.

In my own aircraft, I pulled into a hover over a house where several women and children were huddled on the roof. I could see that they were drenched and terrified but apprehensive as well. I'm fairly sure that none of them had ever ridden in a helicopter, and even for the experienced traveler, standing below a hovering H-34 with the noise of the engine and the buffeting wind from the whirling rotor would be a daunting experience. Being hoisted into the air on a slender cable couldn't be much fun either.

When you're conducting a helicopter rescue, the trick is to hold a steady hover. If you can't keep the aircraft from moving, the evacuee may be injured. I had to look straight ahead and concentrate on keeping my aircraft as motionless as possible. I couldn't see the hoisting activity, but it seemed to be taking longer than usual. There had only been a few people on the roof when I made my approach, so the delay was not anticipated.

My aircraft seemed to be getting heavier, and I noticed that I was right about full power and in danger of settling if more power was required.

"What's taking so long?" I yelled back to the crew chief.

"Sir, we got twenty-eight people on board!" the crew chief replied.

Twenty-eight? Where had they all come from? All I knew was that I was out of power, and there were hostiles in the area. Looking over to my right, I could see a man in lying on a rooftop pointing a gun at us.

"We need to move out!" I shouted.

"The hoist is secured," the crew chief replied. "Let's go!"

I didn't wait for him to repeat himself. We skedaddled back to Da Nang.

The H-34 was designed to carry about thirteen passengers at most. I had more than twice that number on board, and I figured that it had to be some kind of record. I wasn't even close. Captain John Eilertson and First Lieutenant Ron Pettis brought in forty behind me. John and his crew rescued a hundred and twenty-seven people in four or five trips that day.

When I landed, I noticed that I was having some trouble taxiing. A post-flight inspection revealed that my tail wheel was flat. The reason wasn't very hard to spot; it had a bullet hole.

Everybody offered a hand that day, but our combined efforts were not quite enough to save all. The news media reported that more than fifty thousand houses were destroyed in three provinces, and that more than forty-five hundred civilians were dead or missing. Another twelve-thousand-odd-something Vietnamese were forced to seek refuge at government centers in the wake of the flood.

Still, it was a "feel good" moment in the middle of a war in which people died every day.

Later, the aircraft manufacturer Sikorsky awarded all of us with its company's winged *S,* which is bestowed on pilots and aircrews that conduct rescue operations using Sikorsky aircraft.

We often launched out of Hue Citadel, flying troops into battle from the ancient walled city on the Perfume River north of Da Nang. I remember one such mission vividly. The call to load up meant that speed was imperative, and when it came this time we jumped in our cockpits and started our engines.

There was no time to hesitate. We needed to place our troops in position as quickly as possible, so they could accomplish their mission with the least amount of casualties. There were half a dozen birds assigned to this mission, each filled with highly trained Marines whose mission was to engage the enemy with malice. Quickly, we lined up and took off, staying low to avoid detection.

The lead aircraft released a red smoke grenade at the landing zone, so we could see the wind direction and land into the wind. We landed quickly, unloaded, and—just as quickly—vacated the area back to Hue, to await extraction.

The instant we landed and shut down, someone shouted, "Corpsman!"

I hadn't heard any ground fire, but obviously someone had been hit. Everyone rushed to the aircraft where the cry had sounded.

When I got to the aircraft, I saw Captain Walt Ledbetter half-lying in the cabin door, in obvious pain. The rest of us were crowding around to see where he had been hit.

I had known Walt since my days at HMM-363. I can't say we were personal friends, because Marine Corps captains aren't normally friends with second lieutenants, but I had a great deal of respect for Walt, and I looked up to him as a mentor.

He hadn't deployed with HMM-365. He was now attached to the air wing group in Da Nang, and occasionally flew with my squadron to keep up his flight hours and to collect flight pay. Watching him now, writhing in pain, I realized that he might have pushed his luck one time too many.

Then, I caught sight of Walt's injury, and I realized that he hadn't been shot. What the hell? I couldn't believe what I was seeing!

Apparently, Walt had been relieving himself near the tail wheel of his helicopter when the order had come to mount up. Our flight suits had huge zippers from top to bottom, and—when the call came—Walt had jumped and yanked up the zipper, along with a few inches of his "business." The skin on his most sensitive body part had been interwoven in the zipper, and there had been no way to get free and no time to cry about it. Walt had flown the entire mission in that condition, without saying a word.

Walt was a good guy, and we were asked to show a little respect for the personal nature of his injury, and to go about our business while the corpsman worked on him. The only option the corpsman had was to pull down the zipper with a pair of pliers, which may have required morphine for most people, but I think Walt was too embarrassed to quibble. He endured the ordeal and was left with a painful injury. I was just glad it wasn't more serious because sometimes tragedies did occur.

He went on with an honorable career and retired as a lieutenant colonel. Uh, Walt did not get a Purple Heart. He should have, in my opinion, but he probably didn't report the incident. I don't mean any disrespect to those who have received this prestigious award. The Marines of HMM-365 earned eight

Purple Hearts. Most recipients had serious wounds, and some did not even live to accept the honor personally.

I believe the death that bothered us more than others was a young Navy corpsman attached to our squadron who often accompanied us on dangerous missions in case anyone was injured. HM3 Daniel J. Bennett was very hard working and dedicated. He volunteered more than he was assigned. On his last day, he ran from his helicopter to assist a wounded marine and was hit just below the armpit as he was climbing back on board. The wound was fatal, and he never regained consciousness.

I had great respect for all of the captains and majors in our squadron. These were the people who made me a better pilot, and their lessons probably saved my life more than once. Some, in particular, I will remember for the rest of my life. Adnah K. Frain was nicknamed "Hondo." Everybody called him by his nickname, and he had a way of commanding respect without demanding it. I don't believe he had an enemy in his life. He was a true leader and came back to Vietnam a second time as the commanding officer of an A-6 squadron. George Boemerman came back with him, and both were exceptional pilots. More important, they were exceptional human beings.

While aboard ship, between tours to Vietnam, we conducted landing practice while underway. On one occasion, I was flying copilot with Captain John C. Williamson, who was nicknamed "Bear" and bore a striking resemblance to the actor Jeff Chandler. I was having some trouble gauging the speed of my landing approach and came in too fast. The air boss complained to Joe Koler about my reckless speed. Needless to say, I got called on the carpet.

I was standing at attention in front of Colonel Koler, when Bear barged in.

"Colonel!" he said. "Al is a HAC, and he's not used to flying in the copilot's seat. We were working on a maneuver, and that's the reason he was coming in hot."

You see, the pilot in command (PIC)—sometimes referred to as the "helicopter aircraft commander" (HAC) in helicopter jargon—sits in the right seat of the helicopter, whereas in a fixed-wing aircraft, the PIC sits on the left. Landing on a ship, whether in a fixed-wing or a helicopter, is always conducted in a left-hand pattern. In other words, you fly downwind in the opposite direction of landing, with the ship to your left, and then you turn left (into the wind) when you make your approach. But a helicopter does not land parallel to the flight deck. At the ninety-degree position, you turn left, come along the side, and slide into a hover over the landing spot on deck. If you are sitting on the left side, then, you have to look past the PIC to see where you are going on the final stage of the approach. It's not impossible to do, but it's difficult.

The Colonel smiled and told me I was off the hook but to slow it down from now on.

I really had been in the wrong, although not intentionally. My approach had simply been too fast. That's the truth of the matter, and I think Bear and the skipper both knew it. I learned a lesson, but I have never forgotten the gesture.

Bear came back to Vietnam for a second tour in a C-130 squadron and was killed in a midair crash just off the coast near Da Nang.

It was his name I looked for many years later when I visited Vietnam Veterans Memorial Wall in Washington DC. It had been his time. I knew that. But it was hard to see his name up there. I'd had to sit there for a while before leaving.

I was involved in one search and rescue operation while with HMM-365, and it happened near the end of our tour. Initially, only senior captains were assigned to search and rescue operations (SAR), but usually nothing ever happened, and it was boring just sitting around. So it soon became a job for lieutenants.

SAR North, as it was called, was in the northern portion of I-Corps, in a village named Quang Tri near the DMZ. An H-34 was stationed there all day whenever aircraft from the carriers were bombing North Vietnam. We never saw the aircraft going into North Vietnam, and we couldn't hear the bombs going off; it was too far away. We'd bring books to read, get our hair cut, dine on hot food for a change instead of C-rations, and sit around shooting the bull and monitoring the guard channel in case someone was shot down. So far, it had never happened. That was about to change.

Henry Heinzerling and I were in one bird, and Chuck Swan and Pete Mack were in the other. I was the senior aircraft commander, and as soon as we arrived, we settled in for a long wait.

We had just gotten settled when the call came in to saddle up and head north. Head north? We were *already* north! Farther north meant North Vietnam.

We were given a frequency and were briefed as soon as we were airborne: a Navy A-6 Intruder had been shot down. The USAF rescue helicopters had tried to rescue the two-man crew, but the armed escort had been shot down as well. They had been able to rescue the escort pilot, but weather had prevented them from rescuing the A-6 crew. We were being vectored to an area where they thought the A-6 had gone down.

When we were airborne and crossed the DMZ two Douglas A-1 Skyraiders joined us for close air support. We couldn't follow a direct course, because we continuously had to deviate due to fog, and clouds so low that they reduced visibility to zero. We finally had to turn back to refuel, but I wasn't going to quit. As soon as we refueled, we headed north again.

Henry was doing a brilliant job with the map, if you could even call it a map. There were hardly any markings. I think it must have been something the French had left behind many years before.

In some cases, we were barely above the tree line, and Chuck, I'm sure, was having trouble keeping me in sight. The airborne command post had established radio contact with both of the A-6 survivors by this time, and continued to vector us toward the mark, even as we continued to deviate for clouds and fog.

Winding and twisting through narrow valleys, we finally came upon a small clearing with a village to one side. Flying low, we received a hit to the fuselage from ground fire. We could see the A-1s circling overhead. The clearing was so small the A-1s had to continually turn hard to maintain position and I could see condensation trails coming from the wing tips showing the strain on the aircraft necessary to stay within the clearing.

Now in radio contact with the survivors, I asked whether they could see me. One confirmed he could, so I asked him to show himself so that I could come get him. He told me he was hiding in the bushes and was not about to show himself.

I pondered for a second. We couldn't stay here very long, or we would end up on the ground, shot down like him. I asked him whether I was close to his position, and he said yes. So I told him I was going to land and then he could come to me.

As soon as I touched down, I could see him hightailing it toward me from the tree line. I moved closer to him, let him on board, and lifted off.

Chuck was overhead, acting as SAR for me while I made the pick-up. As soon as I was airborne, I told Chuck I would act as SAR for him while he went for the other pilot.

Chuck didn't have any trouble finding his man, and soon we were both headed south as fast as our H-34s would go, which wasn't fast enough in those circumstances.

I met my survivor a year or so later and he told me that he'd had to spend several weeks in the hospital for injuries he'd received bailing out of his aircraft. I don't know how he was able to run like he did to get to my helicopter. It was pure determination and guts on everybody's part. None of us were going to quit, including the downed survivors and the A-1 Skyraiders, and I believe that's what saved us then and many times later.

Chuck and I were awarded the Distinguished Flying Cross, although I didn't receive mine until almost a year later, which was okay, but we had been a two-man crew and each of us had contributed. Pete Mack and Butch Heinzerling each received only a single-mission air medal. I feel they deserved the DFC, along with Chuck and me. For the first time I could remember, I had gotten the long end of the stick. I was uncomfortable about it then, and I'm still not happy about it. If this book does nothing else, I hope it prompts readers to realize that Pete and Butch deserve more recognition than they received.

Allen Cates, Henry Heinzerling, Robert McEachran Tent City Da Nang 1965

Shortly after that mission, the squadron rotated back to Okinawa and prepared to go home. It was going to be a long war, and I told my dad so when I got back to the States. I don't believe he understood what I was telling him and actually was uncomfortable with my claim that we would remain in Vietnam for many years against a relentless enemy. From my observations, we were underestimating the resolve of the North Vietnamese. The attitude I had observed by Americans was that our technical expertise would not be hindered by a soldier who walked through the jungle with a handful of rice and a rifle. After all, we had airplanes, helicopters, tanks, ships, and gobs of bullets, rockets, and bombs. Our adversary was conducting guerrilla warfare against a superior force. Yet, from what I had seen, I was sure the North Vietnamese would not quit until they had achieved victory.

But even then, how could they possibly win? It wasn't impossible. In the *Seven Pillars of Wisdom: A Triumph* by T. E. Lawrence, a small group of Arab guerrilla fighters, against all odds, constantly disrupted a valuable railroad supply route and created a situation in which an army was necessary to keep the route open. The Vietminh defeated the French Republic at Dien Bien Phu. How? The lessons learned are clear and concise: you don't have to like your enemy, or agree with his ideology, but respect your adversary's ability and know the reasons for his tenacity and resolve. Only then can you hope to defeat him. Act indifferent, aloof, or pious and sanctimonious, and you will lose.

Military historian Martin Windrow wrote that Dien Bien Phu was "the first time that a non-European colonial independence movement had evolved through all the stages from guerrilla bands to a conventionally organized and equipped army able to defeat a modern Western occupier in pitched battle."

Are we making the same mistake now in the Middle East? There is evidence to support that theory. In terms of financial expenditure alone, America has spent a huge fortune and the gains are questionable. As such, the wars in the Middle East have greatly weakened America's financial independence, and unless we come to grips with our sworn enemy, the unthinkable could happen and America could fall.

Before we left Vietnam, I got an opportunity to apply for regular officer. Most of the lieutenants were active reserves, and so was I. My application was accepted, and I planned on making a career with the Marines.

Despite my career plans, however, I could not reconcile myself to what I had seen in Vietnam. It was a beautiful country, filled with some equally wonderful people. I didn't know what the future held in store for them, but it didn't look good.

I couldn't see any future in remaining a helicopter pilot either. I asked the skipper if he could exert any influence to keep me from being sent to the training command to teach helicopter flying. That was where most of us were going, although some ended up at Saufley Field teaching primary in the T-34.

I really don't know whether the colonel influenced things or not, but I received orders to report to Marine Air Group (MAG) 36 at Marine Corps Air Station (MCAS) Santa Ana.

When I heard the news, I smiled. MCAS Santa Ana was awfully close to El Toro, the marine jet base.

THE END OF MY MARINE CORPS CAREER

My sister, Beth, was getting married about the time I was to arrive back in the United States. If I hurried, I could just make it. I didn't waste any time. As soon as we landed on the West Coast, I left for Missouri. I made it just in time, thin and somewhat jaded from my Vietnam experience. No one asked any questions about my experience, which was good, because I didn't have any answers. It wasn't that I didn't want to talk about it. I just wouldn't be able to put it in words they could understand. Not then and not for a long time.

While in Vietnam, I'd had the fortune of being taught how to play poker by my good friends Gene Rainville, Caldy Caldwell, and Dan Hamilton. The games were played in a tent just beyond the mess tent. Dan and I still get together, and I enjoy his company now as much as I did then. At any rate, all three of these guys were quite willing to take my money in return for showing me the rudiments of the game, and—like a fool—I allowed them to get away with it.

After a couple of days resting up at home, I went looking for a car. I wasn't sure what kind I wanted, but I had an idea of what it would look like. I stopped off at the Pontiac dealership and immediately spotted a black Gran Turismo Omologato, better known as a GTO. The car looked like it was doing 120 miles per hour sitting still.

Oooooh, what do we have here? I was thinking.

Opening the hood revealed a trio of two-barrel carburetors sitting on top of a 389-cubic inch engine with 360 horsepower. A four-speed standard transmission with a floor-mounted Hurst shifter transferred power to the rear wheels. The tires were Uniroyal Tiger Paws, outlined with a thin red line stripe.

The car had my name written all over it. I was trying not to look like an idiot, and probably not doing a very good job of it. Brand new, it cost three thousand dollars. My poker-playing friends hadn't got all my money, and I had enough for a down payment.

I don't remember bargaining on the price of that GTO. I wanted it, and the dealership knew it. I went off the lot sideways, running through the gears. When I stepped on the accelerator, the engine sounded like it was going to suck the hood right into the carburetors. I broke it in on the drive back to California.

It had only been a year since I'd left MCAS Santa Ana, but when I returned, that year suddenly seemed like an eternity. The base now looked like a ghost town. Everybody had left and gone to Vietnam, and there was a single aircraft on the ramp: a VIP-configured H-34.

I checked in with Captain Blackburn, whom I had met when I'd been attached to HMM-363. There was no squadron and no job for me.

I thought, perhaps, this was a sign. Once I got settled in, I drove over to El Toro to see if I could get a ride in a jet. There was a hop going out with two F-9s, and I was welcomed to come along in the backseat. They found me a G-suit and an oxygen mask, and off we went.

They decided to show me a few tricks. For about an hour, we conducted simulated dogfights with altitudes ranging from 10,000 to 20,000 feet in short order. To boot, I wasn't used to wearing a G-suit. I was breathing in when I should have been breathing out and relaxing when I should have been tightening up. It was like taking a roller-coaster ride on steroids. You could hear the whistling of my sinuses while I was trying to unblock my ears from all the abrupt altitude changes.

They thought it was funny, and I accepted the joke with good humor.

But it didn't change my mind about what I wanted to do. I was determined to fly jets.

But there was just no way. A major told me gently that he couldn't get his own brother into the jet pipeline right now.

I went back to MCAS Santa Ana and realized I was stuck on a base with no squadron and no aircraft. To top it all off, I wasn't completely sure the Marine Corps even knew where I was.

A week or so later, I went out to the beach one night and saw some fairly large breakers coming in. The waves on the West Coast are not usually so large, so I decided to sit there and watch. The breaking waves produced a luminescence that pierced the darkness like a kaleidoscope. I could smell the salt breaking out of the foam, and see small crabs scurrying back into the melt as the water receded. I stayed there for a long time, with my knees under my chin, feeling the dampness seep into my clothes. I slowly realized I was at the wrong place at the wrong time. There was nothing here for me and I needed to go, but where? I felt like I had been thrust back in time to that dirt road in front of my parent's house in Missouri five years earlier staring truth in the face.

The next morning, I asked Blackburn if I could transfer to the training command and, if possible, request to teach the T-28 program. He thought it could be arranged, and a couple of weeks later, I was heading east in my GTO. My new orders were to NAS Whiting Field, where T-28 training was being conducted.

My primary job was teaching formation flying, and I enjoyed it. Gunnery was no longer taught, which was disappointing, and field-carrier training had limited slots, reserved for pilots who had fleet carrier experience. So I was left with a choice of basic training or formation training. I chose the latter. Still, I couldn't shake the uneasy feeling that I was going nowhere and had a lifetime to get there.

My legal training provided me with a secondary position as the squadron legal officer. I actually did more legal work with VT-3 than I had done with HMM-365, and some of it was pretty interesting. I acted as a defense counsel in some cases and a trial counsel (prosecutor) in others.

The cases were all special court-martials, since you had to be an attorney and a member of the Bar to defend or prosecute in a general court-martial. The judge advocate general evaluated all of our cases, and none of mine were ever overturned. I believe the experience helped me later, when I became a business owner, since most of my work was quasi-legal and never went to trial. That's about how it is in the outside world too.

Later, I was transferred to night flying, and when all the students were in, I would dive down to the field at 250 knots, break hard at the center of the airfield, release the speed brake, drop the landing gear, and land precisely on the end of the runway. But, the euphoria of the experience would quickly dissipate when driving back to my rented house at night, and I would soon discover that Santa Rosa County was not as dry as people thought. With a knock and a wink, a bar could be found anywhere, with lots of people to help me forget my loneliness.

What was it that I really wanted? And why was it so elusive?

Many of my old squadron mates had separated from the service and gone to work for the airlines. The idea was to work until you were sixty and then retire. The fortunate ones chose American Airlines. The unfortunate chose Eastern, Pan Am, Braniff, or Trans World airlines and regretted their decision a few years later.

It was difficult to understand why some people went down a certain road, while others went a different way. Was it destiny, or did God simply blink? If destiny, then why didn't I accept the pleasure of the moment?

I couldn't justify it, but I wanted to go back to Vietnam, where life was easier for me to understand. Everyone who has experienced war detests it, but some keep going back for more, like the proverbial insect to the light. Was it the adrenaline rush? Admittedly, I liked dancing with the devil as long as I could pick the tune.

We were allowed to take the T-28 on cross-countries, just like the H-34 when I was in California, and I went as often as I could. I had more range with the T-28, and I went north and east.

Gene Rainville was teaching helicopters close to where I was stationed, and I got a chance to see him often. He told me that he was separating from the service and had an interview with Air America in Washington DC. I suggested that we fly to Andrews Air Force Base in a T-28, to save a few bucks, and he agreed. On the way, I asked if he wouldn't mind me tagging along for the interview, and he said that was fine with him.

The office was small but neat, and I was introduced to Red Dawson, who would be interviewing Gene. There was also a young African American man there for an interview as a flight mechanic. His name was Willy Parker. So I asked for an interview too.

Gene was hired right away, and he was able to leave immediately because he was a reserve officer. But I didn't hear anything. It didn't look like Air America was interested.

Still, I decided to resign my commission and announced my intention through the proper Marine Corps channels. My resignation was not accepted initially. I insisted, however, and knowing I wanted to fly jets, I was offered a transfer to Meridian, Mississippi, to teach T2 Buckeyes, if I agreed to remain in the Corps.

They were finally offering me jets. Back in my student days, I had begged to go to Meridian and had been turned down flat. Since then, I had tried at every opportunity to find a way into the jet program, but the door had remained firmly closed in my face. Now that I was planning to leave the service, suddenly all things were possible. That didn't sit right with me.

There was one superior officer who seemed to understand what I was going through. Lieutenant Commander Bill Sumrall was a tall, fine-looking man, and a perfect specimen—probably what the Navy would want all of their aviators to look like. There was something definitely unmilitary about Bill's long wavy hair, however, and I could tell that the Navy turned him off. He dressed neatly and did his job admirably, but I could tell he was marking time like I was. Years later Bill told me he had wanted to be involved with the active Navy initially, but they had shipped him off to some remote location to fly an aircraft that was void of style and ambiance. There was no real mission. He couldn't stay, but he couldn't leave, and there was nothing positive about his experience. He would soon leave the service, and the Navy would lose a very good officer.

He and I got along great, and his wife, Jan, was one of the nicest ladies I have ever met. Her southern accent just put icing on the cake.

It was an honor to have Bill invite me to his home, where he introduced me to banana daiquiris, which were a treat. He tried to introduce me to one of his wife's cousins, but she had a problem handling banana daiquiris, and, after holding her head over a barrel while she got rid of the evidence, she didn't seem to want anything more to do with me.

The Marine Corps finally decided to let me go, but now I needed a job. I called Red Dawson and asked him if Air America had any slots available. The helicopter pipeline was full, so I asked if there was anything available in fixed-wing.

Dawson asked me if I had any fixed-wing time, and I told him that I was flying the T-28. He quickly assured me T-28 slots were not available and then demanded to know why I thought there might be.

Sensing he was on the defensive, I quickly got off the T-28 discussion and assured him that I had some C-45 time, not mentioning that it was only that short spell in the training command.

"Let me tell you something, Cates," he said. "They shoot pilots in the head over there. Do you understand that?"

I told him that I was a Vietnam veteran and understood the danger. But I couldn't help wondering just what these people were up to where getting shot in the head was commonplace.

Dawson asked if I was ready to go immediately, and I told him I would be separated in December, which was just around the corner. With that, he said I was hired, pending a background check.

My hire date was December 26, 1966. I already had a passport, and a few days later I received first-class airline tickets on Pan Am to Taipei, Taiwan.

The day I separated from the Marine Corps, I didn't even change out of uniform. Elated about my pending employment, I climbed into my car and drove straight up to Missouri. It snowed that night I got there, and my GTO had a hard time getting traction even on dry ground. It wouldn't go anywhere in the snow.

I left a few days later, and Mom and Dad were not sure where I was going or why. I didn't have a ready answer. I didn't know why or where either, but only that I needed to go.

I'd sold the GTO to my brother, Jerry, for half of what I paid for it, and he drove it to New York, where he worked for some think-tank organization. He wrote to me later and told me he'd sold it.

"Do you realize this thing only gets eight miles to a gallon?" he asked.

I wrote back and said, "Yeah, but gas only cost twenty-five cents a gallon. And look at the thrill."

Apparently, Jerry had traded it in for a foreign car, which made more sense to him but absolutely none to me.

Air America

In the summer of 1959, just after I graduated from high school, President Eisenhower ordered US Army Special Forces troops into Laos, a country very few people had ever heard about. The mission was to secretly train the Laotian military to defend their country against Communism.

Several years later, I met one of the team members from that mission, Reuben Densely, who told me they flew to Southeast Asia in a C-124 Globemaster loaded with gear, but they all wore civilian clothes and the mission was highly classified.

Originally the mission was code-named Operation Ambidextrous and later named Operation Hot Foot. In 1961, the mission was declassified and renamed Operation White Star. After that, military advisors were allowed to openly wear their uniforms. Ben later went on to the aviation side of the Army, was trained to fly helicopters and promoted to Warrant Officer. He served in Vietnam flying gun ships and later was employed with Air America where I met him.

In the summer of 1962, while I was still in flight training, the Geneva Accords were signed, which guaranteed a neutral Laos. Military personnel from all nations were required to depart Laos, but the North Vietnamese did not leave, and White Star didn't really end. There was a public announcement that White Star had ceased operations. In reality, the program went covert. US Special Forces personnel came and went from Laos on a continuous basis over the next ten years, but they were back in civilian clothes.

Marines were sent to Laos in 1960, operating from a base just across the border in Udorn, Thailand. Then in February of 1961, President Kennedy issued orders for all Marine Corps operations in Udorn to be turned over to Air America, supposedly a civilian airline that was now operating aircraft that were not FAA-certified. It was called Operation Millpond, and Marine Air Base Squadron 16 turned over Marine UH-34D helicopters to Air America and set up their maintenance and operations department. As such, Udorn became the official Air America station for helicopter operations in Laos.

Several Marine Corps pilots who had been stationed in Okinawa separated from the service and went to work for Air America. At the time, I knew nothing about Laos and nothing at all about Air America.

The flag carrier for Taiwan was Civil Air Transport, fondly referred to as CAT. The carrier had several aircraft, including a C-46, a DC-4, and a DC-6, but the prize was a Convair 880, beautifully painted with a gold dragon on the side. It was called the Mandarin Jet and sometimes affectionately the Golden Worm. Once a year, employees were allowed to travel free to any one of its numerous destinations in Southeast Asia in absolute luxury.

I was led to believe CAT was a sister company, along with a huge maintenance repair company called Air Asia Company LTD, located in the extreme south, in the city of Tainan. At the time it was not explained to me who was the other sister. There was also another company, operating DC-6Bs, called Southern Air Transport, but Southern Air Transport Atlantic in Miami and Southern Air Transport Pacific in Taipei appeared to be separate companies, and actually were not.

Strangely, all of the pilots for Air America, CAT, and Southern Air Transport Pacific were on a single seniority list. This would mean they were all owned by a single entity, but it would be illegal to have one operating certificate and different chief pilots, yet Southern Air Transport Atlantic's pilots were not on our seniority list, but Southern Air Transport Pacific operated on the Atlantic division's operating certificate. Naturally, at this juncture, I was at the bottom of the list and had no idea who I really worked for. Asking questions, as a very junior pilot, would not have been wise if I expected to stay for a while.

Later, a Boeing 727 replaced the Convair 880. A tragic accident one dark night claimed several lives when the 727 ran into the ground short of the runway at Taipei. The wife of the pilot was among those who died, and the pilot was thrown in jail, compounding his misery. The accident ended CAT's flag carrier status, and China Airlines became the flag carrier practically overnight. This was a huge political upset, as CAT pilots had supported Chiang Kai-shek, the Nationalist leader of the Kuomintang in the civil war in China, and when he was ousted by Mao Tse-tung, the Communist leader who ruled China until his death in 1976. It was CAT who flew Chiang Kai-shek and his entourage to Formosa, later renamed Taiwan.

My indoctrination into Air America in Taiwan included being fitted for a uniform, but not the kind of uniform you would imagine. Mine consisted of dark-gray polyester trousers and a light-gray short-sleeve shirt. I would be a first officer initially, and was provided epaulets with three stripes and a set of wings (minus the star on top, which was reserved for captains). I was issued Corcoran boots, but a traditional hat. I was instructed to wear the hat at all times while in uniform, unless I was actually in the aircraft. A few years later the polyester uniforms, which burned easily, were replaced with long-sleeve shirts and trousers that were fire resistant. The traditional formal hat was replaced with ball caps.

I was then sent to Bangkok for ground training for the aircraft I would be flying, where I was informed that, after ground school, I would be based in Saigon, South Vietnam.

I had a choice between the C-45 and the C-47. I chose the latter, simply because I had never flown it before. There were three of us. Frank Thorsen wanted the C-45. Dick Theriault would be going to Udorn to fly the H-34. I had met Dick once before, when he was with HMM-364.

When I arrived in Bangkok for ground school, I was suffering from jet lag, so I went to bed early and planned to get a good night's sleep. Once again, life had other plans for me. Gene Rainville had heard that I was in town and rode the night train down to Bangkok from Udorn for his scheduled time off. He started banging on my door in the middle of the night with a bottle of scotch, demanding that I get up and hit the town with him.

Bangkok has a smell that is difficult to describe. It's a mixture of decaying ancient buildings, exposed to years of heat and high humidity; sweat; hot oil;

pepper; and a tinge of the fermented fish sauce that's used as a condiment throughout Thailand, Cambodia, Laos, and Vietnam. Few women are more beautiful than Thai women, and they smiled readily with dancing eyes and a sensual swing in their hips that seemed to come naturally.

Of all Asian foods, Thai is probably the most pleasant to the Western tongue, as long as you watched the pepper, and the Thais love pepper. There was an abundance of fruits on practically every street corner, including bananas, watermelons, lychees, rambutans, pineapples, mangosteens, mangos, and some others I'd never heard of. Pork was a staple and prepared in many ways. My favorite was ground pork with spices, cooked in a wok on an open fire, and washed down with fresh coconut juice, straight from the nut.

Gene went back to Udorn and the weekend was over. It was time to go to work and the first order of the day was ground school. Air America's ground school was very thorough and no different than what I had experienced in the military. Every part of the aircraft I was to fly was dissected and explained for several days and the instruction included a written test. By this time, just like when I went to helicopters in the training command, I knew the language and what was expected. I studied, but I knew what to study and had a good idea what would be asked on the test. When we completed our training, Frank and I took a scheduled airline to Saigon. I was anxious to find out what was in store.

Saigon

Looking out over the Air America ramp in Saigon, I saw an aircraft that gave me the sensation I'd had when I first set my eyes on the GTO. It was a single-engine turbo prop, with a long sleek nose. It was designed for short takeoffs and landings, with a long wingspan and fixed landing gear. So it wasn't built for speed, but I immediately knew that this was the aircraft I wanted to fly.

Each program had an assistant manager of flying (AMF), and I learned that Jake Wehrell was the AMF for the Pilatus Porter, the aircraft that had my attention. I looked for him right away and told him I wanted to work for him in that airplane as soon as he would let me.

Pilatus Porter. Photo used by permission of Tom Lum.

Jake was a former Marine jet pilot and a great guy. We liked each other immediately.

"Al," he said, "as soon as a slot opens up, you got it."

The first day after arriving in Saigon, Frank and I went to the Air America office in raincoats, because it was, after all, raining, but our rain gear gathered a few snickers from those in the office. We thought we looked cool and clandestine as all get out, but later we realized we were somewhat naïve.

We were informed that our pay would be sent to any bank we designated in the United States and that local currency could be obtained by writing a check. We could live wherever we wanted to in town, but the company had arranged some large villas with several rooms, sort of like bed and breakfasts. We could stay in one as long as we wished or until we found other arrangements.

A flight schedule would be prepared every day and sent to the villas, which provided the aircraft number, designated aircrew member names and departure time. A Volkswagen bus would come pick us up well before the flight, take us to the airport, and bring us back at night.

The C-47s were on loan to the company from the USAF. This did not register with me at the time. American civilian pilots who fly passengers for hire—whether with a commercial airline, a private corporation, or as a charter pilot—must have a Federal Aviation Agency (FAA) pilot's license, and the aircraft must be FAA-certified. It doesn't make any difference whether you are in the United States or not—the law is clear, and violation of that law means immediate termination, and can lead to fines and imprisonment.

Military pilots don't require a pilot's license to fly, however, and military aircraft do not have to be FAA-certified. Most of us earned our pilots' licenses prior to leaving the service, because we qualified for the flight requirements and just needed to pass the test. I think the majority of us anticipated getting flying jobs when, or if, we left the service. Most of the pilots with Air America were former military, but not all. Frank Thorsen had never flown a military aircraft, though he was superbly qualified.

The first letter of the tail number designated its country of registry. So, for example, US-registered, FAA-certified aircraft always had tail numbers that started with the letter *N*. Aircraft registered by the Republic of China had tail numbers that started with the letter *B*. The C-47 I was getting ready to fly, however, had no letter. It had only a number, like 949, with no other markings, because it wasn't FAA certified. I later discovered that the tail number was the first three digits of the aircraft bureau number.

On the other hand, all of the Porter aircraft had tail numbers that started with *N*, like N-52L. They were US-registered and FAA-certified. The C-46s carried the letter *B*, indicating they were Chinese registered, but not necessarily FAA-certified. The Caribous only had numbers. The Helio Couriers were marked with the letters *XW*, meaning they were Lao registered, and the 204B Bell helicopters were all *N* registered.

Caribou. Photo used by permission of Tom Lum.

So, just who in the hell *was* Air America and how did they get away with operating military aircraft that were not FAA certified?

All of this seemed strange to me, but I soon was led to understand by those senior to me that it was best just to do your job and keep your mouth shut.

I spent six months as copilot in the C-47, and it was good experience. I had a hard time flying that aircraft initially, because of the tail wheel. I was all over the runway on takeoffs and scared witless on landings. Finally, Felix Tidwell, the AMF for that program, either out of kindness or out of just being tired of watching me manhandle the aircraft, grabbed me by the shoulders and said, "Al, drive it like a truck."

"What do you mean?" I asked.

"Quit steering it with rudders, brakes, and differential power. Turn the yoke, just like you would driving a truck, and keep it going straight down the runway."

A lightbulb came on, and dammed if it didn't work.

We had to be up at four in the morning for the early flights. The kitchen wasn't open that early, and there was no place to get breakfast. B. P. Pratt, a C-47 captain and retired USAF pilot lived in a villa with his wife, who always packed him a lunch, which he would kindly share with me when we flew together. But it wasn't fair to sponge off a fellow pilot and take advantage of his kindness. It was apparent I needed to find a way to fend for myself.

On those flights, we carried everything from people to live pigs, and we went north to Da Nang, and Nha Trang, and south to Can Tho, and every place in between.

Air America in Saigon was essentially a commercial carrier and even though we were flying aircraft that were not FAA certified, we still acted as if it were a legitimate fly-for-hire airline. Therefore, we filed a flight plan with the Vietnam aviation authorities, received a clearance from the tower with specific instructions as to route and altitude, and flew the designated altitude and route in accordance with that clearance. But we did not have transponder equipment that allowed ground radar stations to see us on their scopes. To make matters worse, all of our radios were VHF, while the military used UHF, so we never knew if we were in the same airspace with another aircraft unless we ran into each other. We looked out for each other within the company by monitoring a common frequency, and had to report to the base by radio every thirty minutes so that operations could keep track of us. Still, we didn't have contact with the military aircraft, and they were everywhere.

The military had also removed every navigation aid except the Auto Direction Finder (ADF), which was antiquated and out of place even in that era. The ADF instrument had a needle that pointed to a radio station. You could follow the needle to the station, but you did not know exactly how far you were from that station until you flew over it and the needle switched ends showing you were now flying away from the station. There was a procedure where you could fly 90 degrees from the station and time how long it took to go through so many degrees and then calculate your distance, but it did not consider wind and was not very accurate. You could also fly an instrument approach using a let down template, where you usually crossed the station at a prescribed altitude and heading and fly out bound for a specific time and then do a 90 degree turn left or right while descending, hold that heading for one minute and then perform a 270 degree turn in the opposite direction. In this manner you could maneuver the aircraft so as to come toward the station located at the airport on a specific radial as shown on the compass with the needle hinged in the center.

The problem was ADF stations were not located on every airport in Vietnam, and many would go off the air in the middle of your approach. Some were very weak and the truth was to really be proficient you had to practice ADF approaches often. We could hear the commercial jets high above us and would ask them to relay our position, which we could only guess at. It worked, but not all the time. Air America captain Bruce Massey slammed into a mountain in a Volpar, a turbo version of the C-45 with tricycle landing gear, killing everybody on board. This might not have happened if his aircraft had been equipped with proper navigation equipment.

There was no way to file flight plans to outlying fields. Consequently, we took what I called calculated risks, dodging through cloud-shrouded valleys at low level altitude, hoping we didn't get shot down or run into someone coming the opposite way.

After a certain number of hours, the big airplanes needed heavy maintenance, and this was conducted in Tainan, Taiwan. We ferried them from Saigon, stopping in Da Nang for fuel, and then on to Hong Kong for more fuel before flying to Tainan. This was all done by time and distance dead reckoning, because the ADF would not work once we were out of sight of land. This was the kind of flying pilots had done back in the thirties.

Volpar. Photo used by permission of Tom Lum.

Then in 1969, Howard Kelly and Milton Matheson took off from Hue in C-47 number 949, heading south for Da Nang. I had my own strategies for making that particular flight. Usually, I would climb into the clouds, fly east by dead reckoning, and let down over the China Sea. I then could follow the coast south to Da Nang by watching the waves break onshore when visibility was low. There were other aircraft down there with me, so I had to remain vigilant. Another of my strategies, which was safer when visibility allowed it, was to fly over the mountains through a pass.

Howard was a retired USAF pilot who knew his trade well. He also had ample wartime experience. He had been shot down during World War II and walked out over the Pyrenees. Milton was also retired with twenty years of piloting expertise. He had only planned to fly with Air America for three years to finance an ice cream store that he and his wife intended to buy to augment his retirement income. Howard and Milton were both good pilots, but that didn't save them. Their flight from Hue to Da Nang was cut short when they flew into the side of a mountain, killing everyone aboard their C-47.

I had flown often with Howard in the C-47, so his death was saddening to me. He and people like "Boo" Howell, Joe B. Henson, "Ham Fat" Connelly, Bill Huff, and Billy Paul Pratt (who had huge hands that looked like little animals attached to his wrists, but a heart of gold), taught me a lot about flying. And, as it turned out, I would need the education.

A slot opened up in the Porter program six months later. Again, I was back in ground school, and then it was on to primary flight training and line training before I was finally released to be on my own.

The Porter was amazing. The prop had reversible pitch, and you could land on a dime, although not quite as short as in a Helio Courier. Norm Owens and Stan Smith argued over that point, and they decided to have a contest at a small field called *Buon Ma Thuot.* Norm went first in the Porter, and as soon as he touched down, he slammed on the brakes. The tail came up, causing the prop to touch the runway, but he landed short nonetheless. He landed right on the numbers painted on the first part of the strip, which designated the runway heading in compass degrees. It didn't seem possible how Stan could possibly beat that landing.

Bell 204B. Photo courtesy of Tom Lum.

Stan was pretty good at these contests, however, and he took advantage of the fact that people didn't clearly work out the rules before acting. There was a small section just in front of the numbers that wasn't runway, but just a concrete strip used as an emergency overrun. Stan landed on that portion with the Helio and won the contest.

I wasn't there to see the actual contest, but I checked out the story thoroughly and am confident that it happened just as I have said.

On another occasion, Stan bet Dave Kendall, a Bell 204B pilot, that he could fly the Helio slower than a helicopter. That was pretty far-fetched to Dave, so he took the wager for a thousand dollars. The Helio had leading edge slats that would bang in and out in slow flight and change the shape of the wing. This allowed the Helio to fly at an extremely slow airspeed, but not as slow as a helicopter. Or, so Dave thought. Again, Dave should have clarified the rules first.

The only restriction was they had to maintain level flight, and not gain or lose altitude. On the day of the contest Stan climbed to 10,000 feet and Dave dutifully followed him. However, at that altitude, Dave's Bell helicopter had to maintain forward airspeed in order to sustain level flight. If he slowed down, his helicopter would settle, and he would break the rules of the bet by not maintaining level flight. It quickly became clear that the Helio really could fly slower than the Bell 204B, at least at 10,000 feet. Dave flew as slowly as his aircraft could manage at that altitude, but Stan Smith's Helio fell behind. As he reluctantly passed the Helio, he saw a grinning Stan Smith, who was holding his hand up, rubbing his fingers, and mouthing, "Where's the money?"

Air America H-395 Helio Courier

Permission to use from The University of Texas at Dallas History of Aviation Collection

It wasn't all fun and games though, and the majority of the time it was deadly serious. Like the C-47, the Porter's only navigation aid was the ADF, and VHF was the only communication radio. We would land at airports all over Vietnam, often at the same time as military pilots. Although the tower talked to both the military pilots and us, we could only hear the tower's side of the conversation; our radios couldn't pick up the military traffic. This was both confusing and unnecessary, and, on one occasion, it was deadly.

The military did not know why we were there, and didn't want us in what they called *their* war, although, strangely, we carried military personnel all the time. One of our jobs was to transport a military courier to several fields where he dropped off or picked up classified correspondence.

Air America had several Porters, so any one of us could be flying in one area on one day and in another area the next day. On courier runs, we usually left the engine running after we landed because the courier's duties would not take much time. I would use the time to do paperwork, which involved keeping an accurate log of flight time between stations. The log would be turned in each day, and our flight pay, along with maintenance schedules for the aircraft and billing to the customer, would be determined accordingly.

On one occasion, I was escorting a courier who was an army major to make his rounds to various airfields. We landed at a small airfield east of Saigon and I left the engine running, since, usually, I didn't have to wait long, and I wanted to prevent any problems with restarting, which occasionally happened. There was no maintenance at these small outlying fields, and waiting for maintenance to arrive took several hours—and since courier runs took a full day, with several landings, any delay meant you didn't complete your work. While waiting for the courier, I was diligently recording my flight time from the last destination. In the Air America Porter, the turbo prop engine was quite noisy, and my Porter, as some did, had a cabin door, so I didn't hear the USAF first lieutenant approach the airplane and open the door.

When I looked up, he was pointing a carbine rifle at me and was visibly agitated. I slowly moved the barrel from my face and asked him what he wanted. The major had returned by now and was white as a sheet.

The air force lieutenant, who was an O1E pilot stationed at this outlying field, said I had cut him off in the flight pattern, causing him to deviate and creating a dangerous situation.

It could have happened. There were no towers at these small airfields, and it was each pilot's responsibility to make sure you entered the traffic pattern correctly without endangering another aircraft. I told him I had not seen an aircraft when I'd landed, and he said, no, this had happened the day before. I explained that I had not been flying in this area the day before and told the lieutenant that we had several Porters. I couldn't tell him which of our pilots might have cut him off but suggested that he report the incident to his supervisor. He shrugged and walked off.

I sat there for a moment, coming to a boil. Didn't he understand we were on the same side! I had made captain before this guy was even out of flight school and had already served in Vietnam as a combat helicopter pilot. Yet, he was a commissioned officer and had pointed a gun at my head, which is irresponsible even if I had committed the act he'd alleged. Then I realized what the situation was really all about—he had resented my presence in Vietnam. I shut down the engine and walked inside, with the full intention of whipping someone's ass. Also irresponsible, I admit, but I felt he deserved it. And, regardless, I needed to walk around and calm down a bit before going back into the air.

He was inside, and, when he saw me, I guess he knew my intentions, because he ran around the building. I chased him and yelled at him and demanded to see his superior officer, but he would have none of that and kept on running. He finally exited to another building, and I couldn't find him.

I gave up the chase and walked back to the aircraft. I wanted to tell the major, who was still just sitting there, scared and shaking, that I had been a Marine Corps captain before coming to Air America, not to mention a Vietnam veteran, and that I demanded his support. But I figured if he couldn't step up as a major and do something about the lieutenant while the idiot was pointing a gun at me, talking to him now was probably a waste of time. I distinctly remember seething over the incident while flying to the next field, hoping America's commissioned officers in Vietnam had better integrity than what I had witnessed that day in both of them.

Usually, the Porters would be stationed in Da Nang in the north, Nha Trang in the center on the coast, or Can Tho in the south, and remain there; the pilots would fly for six days and deadhead to Saigon for a day off. The aircraft would remain at either of these stations until heavy maintenance was required, and they then would come back to Saigon. Da Nang had the trickiest flying, because the strips were small and usually not on a hard surface. Some Porters had larger tires for rough runways, as it was not uncommon to land on a strip with numerous potholes filled with water. The large tires helped tremendously, but landing on some of the strips made for a bumpy ride. Nothing like they'd had in Laos, but difficult enough.

We went into Khe Sanh often, northwest of Da Nang, even when it was under siege, and kind of snuck up on the airfield to keep a low profile. On any single day, I would make as many as thirty-two landings and would be dead tired when I quit at night.

We had military mess-hall privileges. Apparently someone had arranged it, but hadn't felt obligated to tell the lower echelon military personnel. So military there resented our presence in their mess hall, and they showed their displeasure by never talking to us and generally acting displeased.

We knew we were being snubbed, of course, but we were usually too tired to worry about it. We just wanted a hot meal before turning in for the night at the Air America hostel, where ten or twelve pilots would stay at one time.

One night, I was walking into the mess hall with Bill Korbel, another Porter pilot, who was also an attorney and a lieutenant colonel in the USAF reserves. It was wet, and we were dodging mud puddles in the road, when a jeep full of Marines came by and intentionally swerved to hit a puddle right next to us. Bill yelled at them, but we were both tired and hungry, and kept going.

The jeep stopped, turned around, and hit another puddle—this time, much larger. We were splattered extensively, and Bill was visibly agitated.

The jeep stopped, and a marine lieutenant demanded to see our identification. Bill refused, and I had already seen enough. It was harassment, pure and simple, and uncalled for. I told them what they could do with their demands.

They then identified themselves as MPs, drew forty-fives, and placed us under arrest. I guessed they'd planned on shooting us if we resisted. They really couldn't charge us with anything, but they kept us at the station and made sure the mess hall had closed before releasing us.

They told us that they would put in a complaint to our company for our refusing to obey a military order to properly identify ourselves. They pointed out that they had jurisdiction over all third-country nationals, which was ridiculous because it was obvious we were Americans.

There was no use arguing, but the next morning I went to the US Consulate and had the charges dropped when I showed proof that we were American citizens and not third-country nationals, which consisted of Koreans and Filipinos.

The incident was resolved and forgotten, but the question remained: Just who did have jurisdiction over us? Who were we, really?

After a year in Vietnam with Air America, and just before the 1968 Vietnamese New Year, I began to get the impression that the country had turned into a large country club. There was definitely a war going on. American GIs were being killed at a rate of about fifty a day, and while Air America operations in Vietnam were not as military-oriented as they were in Laos, we still received hits from ground fire. Poor weather conditions and the lack of navigation aids continued to make flying in Vietnam hazardous and stressful. Yet in the major cities, especially Saigon, a seemingly constant party was going on.

Every city in the country was teeming with civilian contractors, erecting buildings and airports with long, hard-surface runways, capable of handling large commercial jets. The port in Da Nang was being dredged to accommodate larger ships. The cost for all of this construction had to be in the millions of 1960s dollars.

Employees of the United States Agency for International Development (USAID), Civil Operations and Revolutionary Development Support

(CORDS), Alaskan Barge, Dynalectron, Page Communications, RMKBRJ, and numerous other personnel from a variety of civilian contractors numbered in the thousands. Complicated and costly agricultural equipment was being imported from the United States, and thousands of matched female and male pairs of registered and expensive baby pigs were brought in for breeding stock. None of these costly pigs reached their potential because the Vietnamese farmers ate them instead of using them for breeding stock, as intended—and I'm not sure this was done in ignorance. I found that most indigenous people were a lot smarter than we gave them credit for, and the truth was, the potbellied pig, domestic in Vietnam, might have actually been a better piece of pork. In fact, I've heard that we also introduced trichinosis—a disease caused by a parasite—to the area, as it was not present there prior to US involvement.

Farming equipment, such as tractors with state-of-the-art plows and tilling attachments, and large pumps to improve the rice farming irrigation, were imported as part of the USAID program. The basic idea behind these implements might have been good, but there was no gas for the tractors or pumps in the outlying farms. Some programs were successful. Hybrid rice was developed, which dramatically increased the yield.

Yet it was obvious to everybody that the big plan wasn't working. Just like Johnson's War on Poverty, those who could afford to pay for it would take what was offered for free, and those who couldn't pay didn't want it. Potential soldiers paid high-ranking generals to keep from being drafted, and everybody was on America's payroll.

The first time I ever ate prime beef was in Saigon, at a local restaurant. The beef was meant to attract America's fighting troops but was apparently stolen; you could see the purple lettering on the sides of the steaks.

The harbors were filled with ships carrying goods of every conceivable description. Black markets sprang up in open daylight. Air America maintenance personnel would walk along the hastily put-up tents looking for expensive tools, like bore scopes for large radial engines, which normally sold for twenty times what you could buy them for on the black market. As such, there were also two currency rates—the legal rate and the black market rate, which was considerably higher and used by most people.

Representatives from other countries, including the Viet Cong, would come in and buy state-of-the-art military weapons. Likewise, one news group followed a truckload of medical supplies out of Saigon until it disappeared into known enemy territory. It was surreal. You could clearly hear B-52 bombings in the distance over the buzz of music and patrons in nearby restaurants and nightclubs. Meanwhile, these patrons were consuming the finest cuisine and spirits, which, in America, were available in only the most affluent restaurants and clubs—those that catered to dignitaries and the extremely rich. For those of us in Air America, when out in the war zone, the party we'd attended in Saigon the night before was like a dream.

The money-making venture was remarkable, but how could it possibly help to secure peace in the region? Saigon was built to contain about a quarter of million inhabitants, and now, with probably three times that amount, it was bursting at the seams. The local population, upon seeing what was happening, was not impressed, and their lifestyle had not changed appreciably. After all, how would one tasked with explaining the virtues of democracy to a rice farmer in the delta justify the decadence?

When I asked some of the USAID personnel why they didn't complain, I learned that people who complained or wrote negative reports were sent home with no jobs. Soon, it became apparent that positive reports meant keeping their income, and only a fool would kill the golden goose.

In many respects the war in Vietnam ended on January 31, 1968, with Tet Nguyen Dan, the first day of the year on a traditional lunar calendar and also the most important Vietnamese holiday. Both the North and the South declared a truce. But the truce didn't hold, and the fighting started back up in the North, spreading from Da Nang and south through Pleiku in the central highlands and Nha Trang on the central coast like wildfire. Soon, even Saigon was inundated. Automatic-weapons fire broke out in the streets, and came from people we thought were our friends.

I was holed up in my apartment, unable to even poke my head outside. Normally, I used a Honda 250 Scrambler to get to work and back, but there were snipers in the streets, and for the first time anyone could remember, there was quiet all over the city. After about three days, however, I decided to make a run for it. I fired up the Scrambler and headed for the airport. The normally busy street was now devoid of even bicycles.

I was placed on flight duty as soon as I got there, and sent to Da Nang, where it might have been worse. The ordeal finally settled down, but it was an uneasy peace. Many of the people who had written positive reports now had to make some very tough explanations. Technically, the enemy had lost the battle, with hundreds of thousands killed, but in the process, they had broken America's spirit and revealed the truth.

It would take a few years until the party was over, but it was definitely winding down.

There was a plethora of fine restaurants and nightclubs in Saigon, and our days off were a real treat. There was an International House that I and other foreigners frequented with good food and a few slot machines. Once, in the fall of 1968, while having dinner there, I noticed an absolutely stunning girl in a mini-skirt, playing a slot machine. I was smitten. She was beautiful and apparently Eurasian, leaning more on the European side. I approached, but she refused to talk to me, so I left soon after.

Lucette. Photo taken by Allen Cates.

A few weeks later, I saw her again while having lunch at the Cercle Sportif. It was an elite French sports club, with tennis courts, a swimming pool, and an excellent restaurant close to the presidential palace. My roommate, Henry Melich—also a Porter pilot—was seeing another Eurasian by the name of Colette Lebrun, and they were at lunch with me. I pointed to the beautiful girl and asked Colette if by any chance she knew who this lovely young woman was.

"Oh yes," she said. "That's Lucette. Do you want to meet her?"

I nodded. I definitely did.

Udorn and Back to Helicopters

The winding down of the war meant a reduction in flying activity, and I found myself in danger of losing my captain's position. I realized that I might have to go back to being a first officer, an idea that didn't appeal to me in the least. I started looking for alternatives.

It was common practice to take Porters due for heavy maintenance to Vientiane, Laos, where Air America had a large maintenance facility. I had never been to Laos before and asked if I could take a Porter there when one was due for the required maintenance. While there, I hitched a ride in a Porter heading to LS 20-A, now often referred to as a secret CIA base, that was located north of Vientiane close to the Plain of Jars Plateau. Apparently, while flying activity was declining in Vietnam, it was increasing in Laos, though at the time, I didn't know why.

I spent the day as a passenger, landing on various strips. You could hardly call them strips. They were more like landslides with one-way in (going up a mountain), and one-way out (going down a mountain). Some even had a bend in the middle.

You couldn't really land on them; you crashed, with full reverse pitch and both feet on the brakes. If you liked adventure and an adrenaline rush, flying a Porter in Laos would satisfy the requirement; however, you had to be a senior pilot to go to Laos in a Porter.

In my search for other work alternatives, I discovered helicopter pilots were in demand in Laos as well. Air America's helicopter operation was located in Udorn, Thailand, just across the Mekong River from Vientiane. My seniority was more secure in the helicopter program, which meant if I stayed with that program, I was guaranteed to retain my captain's position. Switching programs, on the other hand, would mean going back to an aircraft I swore I would never fly again—the H-34.

By this time, Lucette and I were seeing each other exclusively. We both delighted in eating out, and she was a master when it came to knowing good cuisine. Lucette's mother was Chinese, and her father was Austrian; he had died from liver cancer eight years earlier, at a young age. Her parents had migrated from China to French Indochina after WWII, where Lucette was born. Later, after the French lost their war with the Vietminh and the country was divided at the seventeenth parallel, the family migrated to South Vietnam.

By the time she was two, Lucette's birth country, French Indochina, no longer existed, so her father sent her to France, where she was educated in a convent. French became her primary language. But she was also fluent in Cantonese, her mother's language, and her English was excellent, with a tantalizing accent to boot.

I had a tough decision. I did not want to be away from Lucette, but I also didn't want to be a first officer. I decided to volunteer for the helicopter program and was accepted. So I bid good-bye to my Eurasian beauty and headed to Udorn, Thailand.

Once again, I was in ground school. Every Air America pilot had to go to ground school when transitioning to another aircraft. He then went through primary training to learn how to fly the aircraft, and then line training in the area he was to operate. In this case, 99 percent of my flying was conducted in Laos, or the "Land of a Million Elephants" from north to south.

Lucette and I wrote to each other constantly, and I was not interested in anyone else. Six months later, I asked her to marry me, and she accepted. We were married in Bangkok at the American Embassy, and I brought her to Udorn after a brief honeymoon.

From left, Allen Cates, Bob Caron, Phil Vaughan, and Steve Sickler. Photo courtesy of University of Texas at Dallas, McDermott Library, History of Aviation collection.

Udorn was filled with former friends and squadron mates. A large percentage of Air America's helicopter pilots were former Marines. Dick Theriault, the gentleman I attended ground school with when I first came on board with Air America, was still there. I hit the ground running because the paramilitary activity was intense and it was important to be alert. After several months Dick stopped me once on the flight line and said, "You are just like me, you know."

"What do you mean?" I asked.

"We both got a death wish," he said. "That's why we're here, and that's why you fly into the storm of battle the way you do." He walked away, leaving me with nothing to say. I really knew nothing about Air America when I hired on with them. They said something about paying me, but I didn't give it much attention. Money was not what I was after. Neither was I looking for self-destruction. Despite Dick's suggestion, I don't believe I had a death wish. I was more afraid of doing something foolish than I was of dying, so I certainly wasn't looking for ways to get myself killed. Joe Koler's words to me several years before were difficult to explain to others who thought I went into harm's way without a plan. I knew, and that was enough. Others would have to find this out for themselves.

From 1962 until the war in Laos ended in 1974 the military couldn't go into Laos overtly, so Air America took on a larger military role. The result was even more casualties. One hundred and forty-six Air America crewmembers were killed in action from 1950 to 1973, but 35 percent of those casualties occurred after 1969.

I had spent a lot of time piloting the H-34 but never truly learned how to properly fly that crazy helicopter until I got to Laos. To be truly proficient required techniques that were never explained to me while flying this helicopter in the Marine Corps. In many respects the H-34 was phenomenal and I gained a new respect for it. I also flew with pilots, both senior and junior, who were extremely talented aviators and could do maneuvers with the H-34 I never thought possible. It was an enlightening experience.

Flying with Air America was never routine. Each situation was unpredictable, and it required experience and expertise. You often hear about the "plight of the pilot," and I guess that's understandable. You also hear more about the quarterback than the linebacker, but one can't perform without the other. The same held true for the pilot and the flight mechanic.

There has been very little written about the flight mechanics employed with Air America. The military called them crew chiefs, combat air crewmen, or loadmasters. Nonetheless, their responsibilities were multiple, and—with Air America—they soon became masters of many trades.

The air freight specialist, commonly called *kickers* with Air America, who manhandled the cargo in the big fixed-wing birds, cannot be slighted either. Many of them paid the supreme sacrifice. They had a tricky business, pushing pallets out of the moving aircraft while clinging on for dear life. And enemy gunfire tended to hit the fuselage more often than the cockpit. Being swarmed by terrified refugees couldn't have been a picnic either; especially when the kickers had to make sure the load was balanced at the same time.

But the kickers usually went home at night to lick their wounds. Air America's helicopter flight mechanics performed many of the same duties as the big-bird kickers, but often, after a full day's work, the flight mechanic's job was just beginning. While the pilot went to his quarters to take a hot bath, eat a hot meal, and relax, the flight mechanic was performing scheduled or unscheduled maintenance on his aircraft. Usually this work was conducted outside, with poor lighting and primitive conditions. The incentive to do a good job was part of his work ethic, but he had personal reasons for it also, because the next day he'd have to fly in the bird he had worked on.

In the H-34, the flight mechanic flew looking to the rear of the aircraft—or to where the aircraft had been—but was blind to where it was going. He could only hope that the pilot didn't run out of altitude, airspeed, and ideas all at the same time. He was a flight crewmember, providing another set of eyes and ears, and often aided in decision-making. Yet even so, he was essentially a passenger, forced to accept the consequences of the pilot's actions.

As memories of my helicopter-flying days with Air America flood my mind, I am reminded of many of the flight mechanics I served with.

Harvey Potter and Jim Beardsly died as a result of injuries received in a crash near L-54. Joe Gaculais was their flight mechanic. Joe survived, but he was terribly burned, and it took several months of painful therapy before he was able to return for duty.

Willie Parker, the young sergeant I met in Red Dawson's office when Gene Rainville was interviewed, received excruciating burns on his hand from an accident in an H-34. Many years and many operations later, he still lives with pain.

When Bill Foster was hit with an enemy mortar, or RPG, he received substantial injuries, including a serious eye injury. There were two flight mechanics on board. It was a line-training flight, and flight mechanic Ernesto Cruz was killed. Few people remember the other flight mechanic. His name was Reggie Boston. Reggie received third-degree burns and lost one of his eyes. He was one of the few African Americans working with Air America.

Pat McCarthy died with Bill Fraser in a Bell. Most people with Air America remember the pilot, Ted Moore, who was flying the Bell helicopter near Site 85 and observed the North Vietnamese Colt bombing the site. It was Ted who maneuvered the aircraft into position to shoot the Colt down, but it was Glen Woods, the flight mechanic, who actually did the shooting. Glen was later killed in a bizarre flight accident in which the rotor blade apparently came off in flight.

Montano Centeno died with Jerry Booth in an H-34 on a mountaintop-landing zone overlooking the *Plaine de Jarres*. You can see this site in the documentary *Flying Men and Flying Machines*, in which Phil Goddard, Assistant Chief Pilot, lands a Bell 205. It was a difficult site for the H-34 because it was high, small, and usually windy. And, as mentioned earlier, the aircraft caught fire easily and burned furiously.

Flight mechanic Fred Alor died from a blade strike while fleeing an aircraft after it suffered a hard landing that collapsed the landing gear. It has been speculated that Fred, who had seen what had happened to Joe Gaculais, was so afraid of fire that he failed to wait until the blades had stopped rotating. While alive, Fred always looked like he was performing in a military parade. His uniform was sharply creased and perfectly fitted, and he always wore an infectious smile. He was very pleasant to work with. His death saddened everybody.

Lowell Pirkle died performing a service for his country. He too was a flight mechanic, and he could not have seen the RPG that exploded in the crew compartment of his aircraft at a site near L-54. The pilots escaped, but Lowell and a Laotian military officer were killed instantly. Lowell's remains were not recovered for many years.

His wife, Debbie, insisted on a burial at Arlington, and she wasn't going to take no for an answer. The request was initially refused, until, incidentally, it was discovered that Lowell had been wounded in Vietnam while serving in the Army. So although Lowell had died in battle with Air America, he was granted burial in Arlington only because he had been wounded in the army. Were it not for that particular stroke of luck, Debbie would have been forced to pay for his burial and for the shipment of his remains to the United States.

I was one of several former Air America employees who attended the ceremony for Lowell. The precision of the pallbearers, the gun salute, and the sounding of taps had a sobering effect. We were acutely aware that we were surrounded by history, tradition, and honor. We could feel it, as if it were tangible.

I'd like to believe that the honor bestowed upon Lowell Pirkle was shared by the other flight mechanics that died or were wounded. But then I also believe that such honor should go to those who did not receive physical injuries. After all, no one was closer to the wounded, the dying, the wretched, and the poor than the flight mechanics. They saw it firsthand—smelled the blood and felt the pain. There was no way for them to escape unscathed, even though the scars were not always visible. I know that these memories will be indelibly branded in their minds forever.

Still, most of Air America's flight mechanics went on to lead fruitful lives, despite (or perhaps because of) their injuries and experiences. Somehow, many of them managed to overcome the trauma and the tragedy. This represents a credit to their will and constitution.

In 1969, Air America had two types of helicopters. The H-34, which was not FAA-certified or US-registered, was provided to Air America by presidential edict over objections from some high ranking military commanders. Bell 204Bs and Bell 205s were also stationed at Udorn. The Bell 205s were registered in Laos, but the 204Bs were US-registered.

Bell 205. Photo used by permission of Tom Lum.

Twin Pack. Photo used by permission of Tom Lum.

Later, a few of the H-34s were converted with two 900-shaft-horsepower turbine engines, and referred to as Twin Packs. And near the end of the war in Laos, Air America received some CH-47C heavy-lift helicopters. Only the very senior got a chance to fly them as captains.

The CH-47C. Photo used by permission of Tom Lum.

Several Air America helicopter pilots had been working in Laos since 1961, and were highly experienced. In 1964, these pilots were collectively charged with the responsibility of being the primary search and rescue (SAR) force for all military operations in northern Laos. By the time I arrived on the scene, the USAF had taken over this duty, but Wayne Knight, chief pilot helicopter, told me that I was required to assist with any SAR, should I be in an area where a military aircraft had gone down. I was also obligated to monitor the universal guard frequency while flying in case an emergency mayday was issued. These orders were not CIA requirements, but came from the Seventh/Thirteenth Air Force, whose jurisdiction we were under during any SAR situation. Initially, Air America flight crews were required to stand by at LS-36 in northern Laos, which frustrated some because SAR was not a daily routine and crews were paid for flying and not for standby. Later, better communication networks allowed crews to stand by and fly simultaneously because thirty minute check in requirements allowed operations in Udorn to know who was where at any given time should an SAR situation develop in their area.

The war in Vietnam had changed its complexion. America's role of providing fighting men had all but ended, and the lead belonged to the army of South Vietnam. The war in Laos had escalated. However, American ground troops were still forbidden in the country, although the air war had increased significantly.

The road network along the Vietnam and Laotian border was commonly called the Ho Chi Minh Trail. North Vietnamese soldiers and supplies, streaming southward into the Vietnam Delta, had previously occupied it. Now, it was being used to supply enemy troops in southern Laos. Air America simply called it *the road*.

Only a few people had seen it, and those who'd worked the area long enough to know its hazards really did not want to see it. The title, Ho Chi Minh Trail, did not accurately describe the "road," which was actually a network of large roadways that could carry heavy trucks loaded with troops and supplies. It was heavily guarded to the point that unarmed aircraft were defenseless. You did not go to the road unless you absolutely had to, and even then, you knew your life was in jeopardy.

All types of American aircraft were used in the attempt to break the supply chain on the road, and the North Vietnamese reacted accordingly. A large quantity of bombs and bullets were dropped on the trail. The North Vietnamese army took personal offense at being bombed and strafed and responding with 23-milimeter and 37-milimeter guns that could knock down any type of aircraft. Increased firepower by the United States Air Force was badly needed.

One aircraft designed to meet this demand was the AC-130 gunship. By the spring of 1971, eight of these aircraft were delivered to Southeast Asia, with several modifications.

The AC-130 looked like a fire-breathing monster when you watched it operate at night. No one could believe that anyone or anything would dare its wrath. These aircraft were designated with a call sign of *Spectre,* which accurately described its mission and capability. Still, the aircraft was vulnerable and its mission was difficult.

Photo courtesy of Federation of American Scientists

The Easter Egg Hunt

Spectre 22 launched out of Ubon, Thailand, on March 30, 1972, and headed east toward the road. It carried a crew of fifteen.

The attitude of the entire crew was serious and guarded. Another Spectre had gone down the night before, and everyone aboard Spectre 22 knew there had been no survivors. They probably had vengeance on their minds, but these men were professionals and knew their mission was only to interdict traffic on the road, stop it in its tracks, and return home safely. What they did not know was that, tonight, this would be a longer-than-normal mission.

They were hit sometime just before midnight. The copilot looked out his right side window and could see nothing but a sheet of flames engulfing the wing. It was obviously a mortal wound, and he realized, "My God, they've got another one of us."

The aircraft commander made a distress call on the emergency guard radio frequency and ordered everyone to bail out. That was their only option. The copilot, emotionally charged, beat a path through a darkened aircraft and leaped out the back into a black night. He floated down in the dark and hit the ground on the very road he had been strafing.

As luck would have it, there was no visible traffic, and he found cover in some bushes while turning on his survival radio.

An airborne command post scrambled from the Korat Royal Thai Air Force Base and started coordinating appropriate rescue aircraft. The controller on board the command post was David J. Preston and he had a call sign of

King 27. Spectre 1 and Spectre 21 C-130 gun ships were also in the area trying to contact any survivors by radio. At this juncture, it had not been immediately determined how many had survived the bailout, if any.

Spectre 21 provided as much information to King 27 as was available until relieved by Spectre 20. By that time, it had been determined there were survivors, but the actual number was unknown. Spectre 20 then established radio contact with some of the survivors and learned that the aircraft had traveled some distance between being hit and bailing out.

King 27 had started to plan the on-scene operation with the assumption that most had gotten out of the aircraft and were potential survivors. His objective was to start a communication network and night visual search for as many of the fifteen men as possible in preparation for a recovery that night or at first light. Thus began the largest and most complex combat rescue operation ever attempted in the Vietnam War.

King 27 requested multiple FAC (Forward Air Control) aircraft, with a call sign of Nail, to fly over the target area and attempt communication on each of the four rescue frequencies. Then allocating one frequency to each of the four Nail FACs as they arrived on scene, he began a nightlong process of gathering information. Eventually, King 27 made radio contact with all fifteen of the downed crewmembers.

Since the on-scene time for each FAC was limited by his fuel endurance, a cycling of aircraft was necessary. Replacement aircraft had to enter the subject area to continue the operation after being briefed. Concurrently, anticipating a possible need to deliver ordnance on enemy forces, King had obtained fighter-bomber resources to orbit the area, which might compromise the safety of the survivors.

As night progressed and more survivor locations were detected, SAR forces were launched from Nakhon Phanom, Thailand, and Da Nang, Vietnam, in case rescue attempts could be made before first light. These SAR forces included Jolly Green helicopters using Limited Night Recovery System (LNRS) techniques, or night-vision goggles, and A-1 Skyraiders for close air support. Because of the scope of this rescue operation, all airborne resources, including SARs, fighter-bombers, and FACS of all sorts, were made available for the mission. Additionally, Air America helicopter resources were requested to aid in the effort.

Bruce Jachens had been operating an H-34 all day out of Savannakhet a few miles to the north. He had settled in for the night at the Air America Savannakhet hostel when the call came for him to launch south. Bruce was a veteran pilot with Air America, and had been called upon several times to rescue downed military pilots. Normally, though, such rescues were done during daylight hours, and he knew that a night rescue in hostile territory was dangerous—you stood the chance of having to be rescued yourself. Almost all of southern Laos was hostile territory by that time, but going to the road at night meant that, though you might survive long enough to be rescued, there were no guarantees.

Bruce talked it over with his Filipino flight mechanic and, in the end, both men essentially said, "What the hell?" and then headed south in their H-34. Just north of Pakse, they joined up with the H-45 that was crewed by Chuck Frady, Jimmy Nakamoto, and me. We had been working out of Pakse for the past several days.

There was no moon, and the sky was blacker than the inside of a cave. Flying night formation without any reference to the ground was not a piece of cake. Both of our aircraft were ordered to maintain radio silence and just stand by and listen while King 27 coordinated all the other aircraft in the area. This was extremely difficult because Bruce and I could not see each other in the dark, and in this case, "standing by" meant flying in a circle in a virtual inkpot. I quickly assigned Bruce to a specific altitude lower than mine and we orbited using our instruments to maintain position.

King 27 learned that two survivors had exited the aircraft shortly after it was hit, and they were located approximately forty miles east of the main congregation of survivors. King 27 did not know it, but, at this location, these two men were in deep trouble. He also did not know that the rest were in an area of relative safety. He assigned support to this secondary SAR area, to gather as much information as possible. Now they had, in effect, a SAR within a SAR.

Since the threat to the two easternmost survivors on the road was unknown, King decided that as long as their situation was stable, he would concentrate

SAR efforts in the area with thirteen survivors. He would delay the east-side pickups until the primary-area recovery operations were underway.

Now that all the crewmembers had been identified and appeared safe, King decided to wait until first light to pick them up. A night rescue is dangerous and could cause self-induced death and injury. At that point, the two Air America aircraft were told to stand down, so we headed back to Air America's Pakse base to secure for the night.

It was well after midnight by the time we got to bed. We had no way of knowing about all of the preparations that had been made; we just assumed that the USAF was doing its job fine without us.

The nightlong effort, as it turned out, consisted of every SAR aircraft in Southeast Asia, more than a hundred in all. As planned, the Jollies and Skyraiders began the coordinated recovery of the thirteen men located on the west side. It soon became apparent, however, that the men were more closely grouped than originally thought. As a result, the carefully laid plans to divide the survivors among specific Jolly/Sandy teams quickly unraveled. As soon as one Jolly started in for a hover over a known location, intending to pick up one survivor, another survivor would make his presence known in the vicinity by radio transmission.

This happened again and again, until all thirteen men had been safely picked up by at least four different Jollies. It truly was an Easter egg hunt, and with Easter Sunday just around the corner on April 2, it was a blessing as well.

Back at Pakse, Bruce arose early, wanting an early start back to Savannakhet. He breakfasted and had the Air America cook prepare him a bag lunch for later. But before he could leave, Pakse advised him that he and H-45 were needed to rescue the two survivors on the road. Apparently, as soon as the main group of thirteen was in the process of recovery, King had released the east-side recovery and asked for assistance from Air America. A Nail FAC, a Raven, and two Skyraiders were also dispatched to assist. It is not completely understood why the USAF rescue helicopters didn't just fly forty miles east and make the rescue of the remaining two crewmembers themselves. They were armed and we were not. It's possible they were low on fuel after picking up the thirteen survivors, or considered it to be foolish to expose the survivors on board to additional hazards by rescuing the remaining two in case they ran into hostile conditions on the road. We did not question the decision. They asked and we responded. We were duty bound to oblige.

The situation, we learned, was tense and urgent. During the night, a lone pedestrian had been spotted close to one of the survivors, so King had ordered an air strike in that area. King was by now well assured that the enemy not only knew there were survivors on the ground but also had a good idea of their location. It was also probable that the enemy knew someone would come to pick them up—unless the enemy got to them first.

We took off together from Pakse with me in the lead as the senior pilot, continuing with the same crews from the night before—Bruce with his flight mechanic, and I with Chuck Frady and Jimmy Nakamoto. When we were halfway to the pickup zone, Bruce experienced a battery fire. His flight mechanic put it out, burning his hand in the process. Normally, that would be cause for aborting, but the two men agreed to finish the job.

Arriving in the zone, I made contact with both downed crewmembers. No one hesitated. We needed to get in and out as quickly as possible. Bruce held his altitude and acted as SAR for me, while I picked up the first one uneventfully, who turned out to be the copilot. As soon as we were safely up and away, Bruce descended to pick up the remaining survivor, while I acted as his SAR.

Bruce's pickup was more difficult than mine. The survivor had been located near a ledge, and Bruce had to hover over him, in close proximity with the ridge. The elevation was not exceptionally high, but even the slightest amount of elevation decreases the horsepower of the H-34 with its antiquated reciprocating engine. In addition, Bruce could see he would not have benefit of hovering in ground effect, due to the uneven terrain. While hovering over a flat surface, a phenomenon called "hovering in ground effect," will reduce the power required to hover due to the cushion of air that's formed from the downdraft of the rotor system. That's because the weight capacity while hovering in ground effect is far higher than that while hovering out of ground effect. Bruce also had another problem. The survivor's chute was right next to him, and the rotor wash would cause it to billow up into the blades. I usually told the survivors on the radio to get clear of their chutes, but this man had bailed out of an aircraft on fire at night, spent the entire night scared to death he would be captured, and the only thing he wanted to do was get the hell out of there.

Consequently, Bruce had to fly overhead and expose himself to possible enemy fire while motioning for the downed man to get clear of the chute. The noise of the helicopter prevented further radio conversation. Then he needed to manipulate his aircraft with skilled precision. Bruce made his approach into the wind and reduced his airspeed, while simultaneously increasing manifold pressure as he descended. This act required increasing the throttle to 2,800 RPM and offsetting the torque increase with rudder. He could sense that the helicopter could safely hover, and arrived over the survivor with full power but zero airspeed. Now, Bruce had to hold his position while checking to see that his RPM was constant, and that there was sufficient power to prevent settling either into the ridge or onto the survivor.

Such maneuvering required Bruce to be oblivious to any outside activity. He could not be concerned even if fired upon. The safety of the survivor depended upon Bruce holding an exact position.

On cue, the flight mechanic lowered the hoist and collar. Now all that was necessary was for the survivor to place the collar around him and wait to be hoisted up.

The downed man was understandably apprehensive. Most of his adult life had been spent in the USAF. He had been schooled in rescue techniques and knew almost instinctively how to react. But all of his training had come from people in USAF uniforms, using aircraft with USAF insignia. Now, he was looking up at a pilot who could pass for a Russian, and an Asian flight mechanic in civilian uniform. On top of that, the helicopter was obviously antiquated, and was devoid of all visible markings.

You could visualize the man asking himself, "Who are these people? Where are my people?" He was also tired as well as terrified.

Bruce had his hands full of controls and knew he was a sitting duck for anyone with a slingshot, much less an anti aircraft gun. It was time to go, and the survivor had to make a decision quickly.

Both Bruce and the flight mechanic were probably yelling at him to get on, at the top of their lungs, but verbal communication would have been impossible hovering well above him and the engine at full power. There was no way to explain the situation to him. The only thing Bruce could do was look at him and motion with his head to get on. The flight mechanic was at least able to use hand and arm motions, urging the survivor to harness himself.

Finally, reason set in, and the survivor placed the hoist around his body and allowed the flight mechanic to haul him up into the cabin.

Now safely airborne, Bruce joined up with me, and we both headed west for safety.

Then Bruce asked the flight mechanic, "How's our passenger doing?"

"He looks a little white around the gills," the flight mechanic replied.

Bruce reached over and grabbed one of the sandwiches from the lunch that the cook had made for him that morning, and he handed it down to the mechanic. "Give him one of these."

Leaning over to the frightened survivor, the mechanic handed him the sandwich and said with a smile, "Welcome to Air America."

The USAF rescue helicopters with the other survivors were waiting for us at a small but relatively safe outlying field near Pakse. I don't know why they didn't land at Pakse, which was absolutely safe, but it could be they didn't want the public to know they were in Laos. The previously rescued Spectre 22 crewmembers greeted our survivors warmly and with relief. The USAF rescue helicopter crewmembers just looked at us without expression. We never shut down. It was obvious we were not invited to the party and we quickly departed. I went back to Pakse for my next assignment and Bruce went back to work at Savannakhet.

It was this final act that completed the successful recovery of all fifteen crewmembers, a SAR mission that will go down in history as the largest successful aircrew recovery of the war. Yet Air America was not to be recognized.

On the other hand, the pilot in command of the USAF AC-130 is rumored to have received the Air Force Cross, the nation's second highest honor. The Jollies that rescued the first thirteen men probably were decorated as well. And later, although King 27 wrote about the operation and included Air America, when *Stars and Stripes* picked up the story, our part of the rescue was omitted. A March 2009 VFW article described the rescue, but they also omitted Air America. I complained as a VFW member, and they printed a letter saying that we had been there. That was all.[2 3 4]

---

2 http://www.jollygreen.org/Stories/DavidPreston/15_gunshipmen_rescued_from_south.htm

3 http://www.spectre-association.org/images/acphotos/AnthonyBertrand/rescue%20mission.jpg

4 http://www.spectre association.org/library/Articles/VFW_Mar_09/Spectre%20article-page%207.jpg

Typical Air America Work

I was involved with four more SAR events in Laos, but SAR was not our primary job in the late sixties and early seventies, since the military had taken over that responsibility. We were still needed, because we operated closer to the activity than the military rescue helicopters, but our primary work was supporting the Thais and Hmong in northern Laos, and the Lao military in the south. That work varied from doing runs for the US Army's Requirements Office (RO), which mostly involved doing rice-hauling for refugees, to direct war efforts, which included doing medical evacuations and supplying small zones in the mountains with food, water, and ammunition from one end of Laos to the other. RO was hard, but boring to me. I preferred the direct war efforts, where the fighting was.

By the early seventies, Air America now had Air Force C-123s, C-130s, C-47s, Pilatus Porters, C-7 Caribous, C-46s, Helio Couriers, CH47C helicopters, Bell Huey helicopters, and, of course, H-34 helicopters. Most of these aircraft were not FAA-certified. About a year and a half after I got to Udorn, I was able to transfer to the Bell, which was, in my opinion, a much better aircraft. The Bells were better suited for higher elevation because of their jet-turbine engines.

As the war escalated in Laos, Air America's activity escalated as well. Job description for CIA operations involved placing road-watch teams into enemy territory and supplying Hmong troops with ammunition, water, and food.

Air force contracts designated Air America to move huge quantities of ammunition from Thailand into Laos to support secret US military activity. Air Force crews flying C-130s would fly into Udorn and park, and then Air America flight crews took over and flew the birds, loaded with ammunition, into Laos. When they were finished, the USAF crew would come back aboard and fly them home to either Vietnam or Okinawa.

As mentioned, helicopter activity was sometimes mundane with rice hauls to refugees, but near where the war effort was located, the activity was exactly like it had been with the Marines in Vietnam. Pinnacle landing zones were scattered as posts for the fighting troops, and Air America's job was to take supplies in and take wounded and dead out. Very often, this was done under enemy fire, and many Air America flight crewmembers were wounded and killed in action. Weather and mountainous terrain were also constraints, and in the spring, slash-and-burn farming by locals created a dense fog that made it seem like you were flying in a glass of milk.

In January 1972, the North Vietnamese army were trying desperately to close the war in Laos by attacking the secret CIA base in Long Tieng, Laos (LS-20A). The fighting was extremely fierce, and Air America aircraft encountered small arms as well as 122-milimeter rockets and artillery fire. This was the first time I had experienced being in close proximity to a 122-milimeter-rocket blast. I was on the ground getting ready to take off at Long Tieng when the rocket hit about 20 feet from the aircraft. The sound was piercing and louder than anything I had heard before.

On the same day artillery fire close to my position had caused me to abort my landing on a hospital landing zone on Skyline ridge just above LS-20A, but it hadn't been nearly as loud. I had just departed an outpost a few miles away where heavy fighting was occurring. We were hurriedly hauling ammunition in and wounded out, trying to assist Thai troops defending Skyline Ridge. We had to time the artillery rounds as they landed and then lift off with wounded just as the next round came into the landing zone. I could clearly see A-1 Skyraiders firing rockets and dropping bombs onto the enemy who were just below the landing zone. The loss of Skyline could mean defeat for the Hmong and political ramifications akin to what happened at Dien Bien Phu and the French Republic several years earlier. Every effort was being made to prevent that from happening.

At that time, Wayne Knight was the chief pilot for helicopter operations and was in charge of all Air America helicopter crews working in Laos. Wayne was a former marine and had been in Laos since the early sixties. He didn't just fly a desk, and, in fact, often flew upcountry to keep his hand in the game. In March 1972 he and First Officer Michael Braithwaite and Flight Mechanic Bob Noble took off from Vientiane, Laos, and headed north to LS-20A in a Bell 204B. The weather conditions were marginal as usual that time of year, and they had to land at a lower elevation airfield and wait. Both pilots had been briefed on the enemy situation and received situation reports from other pilots in the area. The weather finally cleared enough to allow them into LS-20A to receive instructions from the CIA case officer on duty.

Their job that day would be to sling-load supplies into the various landing zone locations (LZ), wherever troops defending LS-20A were located. All of the LZs in that area had letter designations and map coordinates to enable the pilot to know where he was to go. Certain LZ locations were too dangerous to land in, but the loaders on the ground kept changing the LZ letter designations but with the same coordinates, trying to fool the pilots into taking supplies to troops who needed them, even if that meant a crashed helicopter on their heads. Radio traffic was constantly loud and busy with new situation reports about the various LZs.

The difficulty for the pilot in such a situation was making sure he kept the crew relatively safe in a very unsafe environment. The secret was to try to predict what was going to happen before it happened, and that meant preplanning and lots of it. Unfortunately, the situation was too fluid, making preplans evaporate like the mist. Mindful of the situation, both pilots and the flight mechanic looked for any sign of enemy activity as they descended into each LZ. The work was both tiring and stressful.

Eventually, as it often happened, all the plans in the world wouldn't completely make up for an enemy bent on having his way. And so, just as Wayne descended in an LZ that was supposed to be safe, automatic small-arms bullets tore through his aircraft. Smoke and fire filled the cockpit as Wayne aborted the approach. He tried to call out on the radio, saying he'd been hit, but a bullet through the cyclic control stick had ripped the wires away. Wayne looked at Braithwaite and saw that his face was crimson with blood from multiple shrapnel wounds, although they did not appear to be serious. In turn, looking down, he saw blood and realized he had been hit in the leg.

Fortunately, Wayne was able to get the aircraft back to LS-20A, where both pilots were treated. They'd been lucky. No bones had been hit; they'd gotten flesh wounds only. Many others were not that lucky.

All medical evacuations were handled by Air America-manned helicopters from elevated landing zones in the mountains and often under enemy fire. There were times when pilots were forced to stop flying and wash blood from their decks with buckets of water because they became too slippery. It was often difficult to remain focused because of the carnage. Young fighting boys with missing limbs and, in some cases, missing faces—where shrapnel had removed the nose, mouth, and eyes, leaving only orifices on a living person in terrible agony—were carried from the battlefield to the hospital.

Supporting American Military And Dying While Doing It

The C-123K taxied from the Air America ramp in Udorn down the taxiway, which sat alongside the active runway, to a location on the airfield called Pepper Grinder. There, they shut down and United States Air Force personnel loaded 18,000 pounds of ammunition, which included white phosphorus, onto the aircraft. The pilot in command was Captain George Ritter. The copilot was First Officer Roy Townley. The senior air-freight (AFS) specialist was Ed Weissenback, and his assistant was Khamphanh Saysongkham, who was either Thai or Lao. Captain John McRainey was flying a C-123 K out of Pepper Grinder at the same time. John's load of bombs was designated for Lima Site 20A; George's aircraft was scheduled to fly to Lima Site 69A, which was farther to the west.

Both planes departed and climbed north to the normal altitude of 9,000 feet. The C-123 was not pressurized and remaining below 10,000 feet was necessary because above that altitude the oxygen content is insufficient, but it meant you often flew in the clouds with no visible reference to the ground or the sky. John reached his destination, unloaded, and headed back to Udorn for another load. George's flight path would take him north to where the Mekong turned to the west, and then west to 69A, staying well south of the Mekong and Pak Beng. George and his crew, however, never reached 69A and were never heard from again. John reported later that clouds obscured the ground and that there was a stronger-than-normal wind from the south that day.

The Chinese had been building a road in accordance with an aid contract from the southern part of China. The road ran south through Pak Beng to the Mekong River. It was known that the Chinese had heavy anti-aircraft guns near Pak Beng, but there had been no reports of aircraft coming under their fire. There was no explanation as to why the Chinese needed heavy anti-aircraft guns in a neutral country.

Jim Rhyne, chief pilot of the fixed-wing in Laos, loaded a Volpar (a converted Beech C-45 with twin turbo-prop engines) with leaflets soliciting any information about the crew and offering a reward. He and the senior air-freight specialist, Bobby Herald, riding in the back, then flew to the vicinity of Pak Beng where they thought the C-123 might have gone down and dropped their leaflets. They were hit with heavy anti-aircraft gunfire, and Jim was severely wounded. Bobby probably saved Jim's life by using his knee and holding pressure above the wound to stop the bleeding as the plane hurried back to Udorn and the hospital. His leg was amputated at the ankle, but he healed and with a prosthetic device he eventually returned to flying for Air America as good as ever.

There was no obvious reason for the Chinese to fire on unarmed aircraft, and a complaint should have been lodged. However, an analysis of the historical events of that time period shows that Nixon was making an unprecedented trip to China during this period and that China was soon to become a member of the United Nations. China was shortly thereafter granted inclusion in the United Nations.

A complaint to China would likely have been made if America had openly been in Laos with US military pilots. But China was a key player in the drama of Southeast Asia, as they were in Korea, and the United States was not in a position to complain about a supposedly civilian airline that was illegally carrying ammunition to US troops in civilian clothes in a neutral country.

Mr. Dudley Foster, who was actually a CIA employee imbedded with Air America, conducted in-depth research about CAT/Air America personnel killed in action. It was an exhaustive endeavor that he received very little credit for. I included his report, with his permission, in our application for veteran status. The following information is paraphrased from that report for the period of time from 1969 to 1974, and includes my comments.[5]

- The Chinese shot down another C-23K in March 1973. Captain James Ackley, First Officer Clarence Driver, AFS Chudchai Chiewchengsuk, and AFS Kenekeo Narissak were all killed.
- Flight Mechanic Alfredo Alor was killed in a Marine Corps H-34 helicopter operated by Air America. A rotor blade hit him after the aircraft was forced down by small-arms fire in the southern part of Laos in May 1972.
- Captain John M. Bannerman, First Officer Charles McCarthy, AFS B. Somchai and AFS Suthi Chipaibul were flying a US Air Force C-7 Caribou when 37-milimeter anti-aircraft guns near Saravane, Laos, hit them in November 1972. The aircraft crashed and everyone aboard died. Air America was supplying Laotian troops in the southern part of Laos in a paramilitary role, and the fighting had been very heavy in Saravane.
- Captain Harvey Potter and Training Captain John Beardsley died in March 1970 from burns received in a US Marine Corps H-34 that crashed while supplying Laotian troops near Louang Prabang, north of Vientiane. Flight Mechanic Joe Gaculais was severely burned, but survived, and eventually returned to flying. Joe's burn scars were obvious and extreme. Mrs. Potter and Mrs. Beardsley were quickly packed up and shipped out of Udorn. Both eventually sued the government to get the life insurance promised them when their husbands were killed.
- Gerald Booth and Flight Mechanic Montano Centeno were killed in a US Marine Corps H-34 in July 1969, when it crashed onto an elevated landing zone overlooking the Plain of Jars.

---

5 Employee Deaths: Civil Air Transport, Air America, Air Asia, Southern Air Transport Dudley Foster Collection (Air America Association) http://www.virtualarchive.vietnam.ttu.edu

They were supplying the Laotian troops with food, water, and ammunition.

- Captain Howard Boyles, First Officer Jack Cavill, and AFS Pracit Chaichana, while flying a US Air Force C-123K, were killed in February 1973, after being hit by a missile near Thakhet, to the east of Vientiane and north of Savannekhet. AFS Sourinch parachuted out and survived.
- Captain Herbert Clark was killed in June 1971 after his C-46 was hit by enemy ground fire and crashed. Three of the AFS crewmembers bailed out and survived, but AFS Trikit Thuttanon was also killed.
- In April 1973, Captain Charles Osterman, First Officer Terry Clark, and Flight Mechanic Valeriano Rosales were flying a US Army Huey and were hit by a heat-seeking missile near Huong Hoa South Vietnam. All three were killed and the aircraft was destroyed.
- The C-130 was capable of carrying huge loads at much faster speeds than other cargo aircraft. It was also pressurized, but entry into the airfields in Laos had to be done visually. There were no navigation aids, and the weather in Laos during the spring when the farmers conduct slash and burn farming creates thick smoke making it difficult to maintain visual reference with the ground. Landing at LS-20 Alternate, which was nestled in between two ridgelines, is even more difficult because it sits in a bowl and the smoke tends to settle in low places. There was only one way in and one way out of this airfield, because a limestone mountain called a *karst* was at one end. The C-130s were a big plus in the war effort. They were able to carry many wounded soldiers at faster speeds to the hospital in Thailand, and bring back fresh troops the same day. On this day, however, Kevin Cochrane hit Phu Bia, an eight-thousand-foot mountain peak a few miles east of Lima Site 20A. Other crewmembers aboard included First Officer Robert McKean, AFS Gerald Delong, and

Billy Hester, as well as Training First Officer Huey Rodgers and Flight Engineer Milton Smart.

- In July 1972, Captain Ben Coleman flew into a mountain trying to drop arms to Laotian troops in heavy battle. The weather was bad that day, and the clouds were touching the trees at it often does in the mountains in Laos. The crash also killed First Officer John Grover and AFS Thanom Khanthaphengxay. They were flying a DHC-6 Twin Otter. All of them were highly experienced. Jack Grover, previously a Porter Captain in Vietnam, had accepted a first officer position in Laos when a reduction in activity and his seniority prevented him from continuing as a pilot in command.
- Ernesto Cruz was a highly experienced flight mechanic and often conducted line training for new flight mechanics. In January 1971, he was flying with Bill Foster in a US Marine Corps H-34 and conducting line training with Flight Mechanic Reginald Boston. Either a rocket hit the aircraft or a grenade exploded while they were on an outpost north of LS20A. Ernesto was killed and Boston was severely burned. Captain Foster was also injured and suffered severe loss of sight in one eye.
- In August 1969, Ralph "Cotton" Davis loaded up his Porter at LS20A, took off, and was climbing parallel to Skyline Ridge, adjacent to the runway, when he was hit by small-arms fire and killed instantly. The aircraft crashed and burned and all aboard were killed. Management initially placed the blame on Cotton for overloading the aircraft, but an autopsy revealed a bullet in his heart.
- The Porter was an impressive aircraft. It had a 550-shaft-horsepower turbine engine and a 48-foot wingspan. It could land on a dime and had phenomenal takeoff capability. In Laos, it was used to make airdrops to troop outposts deep in the mountains. It was popular because it was powerful and could operate at very slow speeds, but this capability also made its mission difficult and

precarious in the weather conditions often encountered in Laos. In March 1971, Ben Franklin crashed his Porter into a mountain slope and was killed after taking off from a mud-filled airstrip.

- A sniper round to the head killed William Gibbs in May 1969. He was flying a US Marine Corps H-34 helicopter near Louang Prabang and was taking off from an outlying outpost after delivering supplies to Laotian troops.
- Norman Grammer was flying a US Army Huey and approaching Lima Site 20A when his aircraft crashed after completing a resupply flight. All crewmembers were killed. The exact cause of the accident was never fully explained. A reliable source said it could have been caused by mechanical failure due to pilot-induced mast bumping, while trying to remain in visual contact with the ground in bad weather. It was confirmed that one blade came off the main rotor system and the aircraft plummeted from a high altitude. The flight mechanic on board was Glenn Woods, who had shot down the AN-45 Colt North Vietnamese aircraft that had been bombing Lima Site 85 in 1968.
- Captain William Reeves, First Officer Joel Gudahl, AFS Praves Satarakia, and AFS Thonkham Khammanphet were killed when their C-123K hit a mountain in bad weather near Ban Namm Eui, Laos. They were carrying 12,000 pounds of ordnance and five passengers.
- Captain Howard Kelly, FO Milton Matheson, and AFS Nguyen Van Hanh were killed when their US Air Force C-47 hit a mountain in bad weather just north of Da Nang in January 1969. The C-47s in Vietnam were on loan from the United States military. In addition, as part of Air America's strategy of secrecy, it was common practice for the military UHF navigation equipment to be replaced by incompatible VHF units when the aircraft changed hands from the military to Air America. Howard took off from Da Nang and flew to Hue in the north. In bad weather, there was no way to get back without flying beneath the clouds

along the beach. Unfortunately all aircraft in the region were forced to take the same action, so communication between them was critical to prevent collisions. Because of the incompatibility between the military UHF radios and Air America's VHF radios, however, there could be no communication, so Howard took the safer route and crossed the mountains to the north of Da Nang through a passage. This time, the passage was closed with clouds and Howard and Milton crashed not realizing they were below terrain elevation.

- In March 1971, Kenneth Houp, flying a Porter, was killed when he had a mid-air collision with an Army Cobra. Both were trying to land in Can Tho, in the southern part of South Vietnam, at the same time. This incident was also due to the lack of communication caused by the incompatibility between military UHF radios and Air America VHF radios. It was never explained why Air America, using VHF radios, was operating in a war zone alongside military aircraft using UHF radios, except that the use of VHF radios was part of Air America's covert strategy. Air America was operating military aircraft that were not FAA-certified, but attempting to look like a civilian airline by removing military radios and navigation equipment. It is unprecedented that an airfield with hundreds of landings a day would operate with some on VHF and some on UHF, each unable to hear or speak to each other.
- Jon Merkel was flying as co captain in an H-34 with John Ford near Tha Lin Noi, Laos, in February 1970. A single bullet through the cockpit window killed him.
- In April 1971, Harry Mulholland had a mid-air collision with an Air Force U-17 and was killed. This was another fatal accident caused by Air America's reliance on communication equipment that was incompatible with the military's.
- Lloyd Randell was killed in a Porter trying to land at Lima Site 20A in bad weather, in April 1972.

- Pilot James Rausch crashed in a training accident in 1967, just out of Saigon. He was seriously hurt, but recovered. Later in 1972, he was flying near Ban Houi Sai with a Thai copilot in a Marine Corps H-34. They were delivering a load of food, guns, and water to troops at an outlying field, and ran into enemy gunfire. A single round killed James.
- Frank Thorsen learned how to fly as a civilian. He flew a converted Volpar with turbine engines that were used as a high-altitude radio relay for the US military after Site 85 was demolished. The converted Volpar was also used as a photo- recon aircraft. For hours on end, pilots of such converted aircraft would fly in a circle at 25,000 feet, on oxygen; it was a tedious and thankless job. The photo recon work they did was equally dangerous, but livelier. These missions required two crewmembers and the aircraft were often shot at by enemy troops. That was how, in July 1973, Frank was killed with a single round. I helped Captain Ray Jeffery wash the blood from Frank's personal effects. While doing it I could picture his smiling face the day we met in Bangkok six years earlier.
- Leonard Wiehrdt was a retired Air Force pilot. He started out with Air America flying the C-47 in Saigon. In April 1972, he was flying a Porter near LS69A and ran into the ground. He sustained severe head injuries and probably died on impact.

Spending The Night In The Jungle

War was not constant, and quite often we did routine resupply work to the outlying outposts. Still, the wind and weather often made such work equally hazardous. Over time, flying activity began to diminish, and I was sent back to the H-34 because the more senior pilots filled all the Bell slots, which had also been reduced. To me that felt like punishment, but to be fair there were pilots who really liked the H-34 and didn't want to fly anything else.

Air America converted a few H-34 helicopters. Conversion was done by taking out the radial reciprocating engine and replacing it with two twin-turbine engines. The resulting aircraft was called the Twin Pack, and it had much better performance than the H-34 and even the Bell. I looked at the Twin Pack as my escape route from the H-34, but I was too junior to fly it. However, there was a catch: to be allowed to fly the Twin Pack, you had to agree to fly what was called Special Project. I put in a bid for the position and got it because some pilots senior to me did not want to fly Special Project, as it involved a lot of night flying and more hazardous activity.

While the Twin Pack had a lot more power than the H-34, it also had a couple of quirks, one of which involved landing technique. You landed the H-34 by staying in translational lift and riding the rotor system as if you were on a rope. To do this, you dissipated your airspeed as you descended on an angle, and reached zero air speed and zero altitude simultaneously, touching down on the tail wheel and cushioning your landing on the main gear with residual energy in the rotor system.

The Bell was different. Your approach was much slower, and you hovered in on a shallower angle. At first, I felt I would drop out of the sky in the Bell, because it wasn't possible to land that way in an H-34 at altitude.

The Twin Pack would not land like an H-34. For some reason, the energy in the Twin Pack's rotor system was greater causing the aircraft to float, and I would overshoot the intended landing place if I used the same technique as in the H-34. I had to be much slower in the Twin Pack and land like a Bell, but because the Twin Pack had a four-bladed rotor system, it would lose translational lift early, and the aircraft would shake and shudder like an old dog when landing on a small elevated landing zone.

The other problem with the Twin Pack was that its two engines had to be synchronized through a device called a torque control unit (TCU), and then combined into one transmission to the rotor head. Should the TCU sense an over speed on one engine, it would shut the opposite engine down to flight idle. That happened rarely, but it did happen. The Twin Pack would then fly on one engine if you maintained airspeed, but even at sea level, in a fifty-foot hover, you could not maintain altitude if one engine was shut down to flight idle. When landing on an elevated-terrain pinnacle-landing zone, should one engine fail, you would settle in short of the landing area. You could take off with one engine, but the aircraft had to be light and you had to roll it off on a runway like an airplane.

Every pilot knew to land and take off into the wind, but some pinnacle landing zones were placed in a position where it appeared favorable to land downwind. Landing downwind, however, was a serious mistake, even if the landing was straight downhill (which is uncomfortable). And when landing at night, you had to be very slow on your approach, because your depth perception was not as good. If you overshot, you may not be able to recover in the dark. All of this meant that when landing at a small landing zone in the mountains in Laos at night you needed both engines. This lesson became more apparent later.

In the spring of 1972 I had been asked to go to Edwards Air Force Base in California, along with Air America captain Robert Mahaffey, to fly a specially built Hughes 500P. This aircraft was modified with cryogenic forward-looking infrared radar that enabled a pilot to fly at night, completely blind, using only the monitor in front of him. It had other modifications as well, including a five-blade main rotor system and a special tail-rotor designed to reduce noise.

A few months before that, the aircraft had been used to go into North Vietnam with a crew who tapped into phone lines and thus provided information to American negotiators at the Paris peace talks in regard to what the North Vietnamese were up to. In that same operation, Air America's special project group had used the Twin Pack to perform SAR and to place the tree borne antennas used to pick up the phone signal and relay it back to Udorn. The pilots who had been used in the Hughes had been brought in from the army and were now at Edwards training Robert and me, although neither of us ever learned the full extent of what the mission was about.[6] We trained for two months and were then sent to Air America's office in Washington DC. There we were asked where we wanted to go next.

I wanted to go back to the Twin Pack at Udorn, and Robert ended up in the same place. Once back, we could tell that the war was winding down. Flying was becoming less strenuous. Had I only known what would happen when I returned, I might have simply quit. But quit and go where? In my mind we hadn't finished our work in Laos, and to simply quit was not something I could contemplate. I also wasn't clairvoyant. Besides, Laos, at this time, was my home.

In late 1973, after securing for the night at LS-20A, the CIA case officer referred to as the customer requested that I fly to a pinnacle outpost, extract a critically wounded soldier at first light, and transport him to the hospital in Udorn. I had been landing on that outpost all day and was skilled at night flying, so I told him that I could make the pickup in the morning, but suggested that we do it that night, instead, if the soldier's condition warranted it.

---

6 http://www.airspacemag.com/military-aviation/the_quiet_one.html#

Hughes 500P Photo taken and used by permission of Mr. Shep Johnson.

I cleared it first with Lloyd Higgins, the senior Air America pilot who was present, before proceeding; Air America's policy put the senior pilot present in charge of any decision of this type. I also got approval from my copilot Charlie Basham and the flight mechanic Chuck Low.

This particular pickup location was on a mountain and qualified as a pinnacle-landing zone, but it was twice as large as most, had clear access, and would—I was assured—be well lit. The takeoff from LS-20A was critical, because there were no lights on the runway, but we arrived at the landing zone with no problem.

After making an over flight to check the wind, which was calm, I established an approach paralleling the ridgeline. I slowed down using the energy in the rotor system and continued slowing down while increasing power. It should have been routine. As expected, the landing zone was well-lit, and the landing should have been uneventful. But, as I was adding power on the final portion of the approach, the aircraft suddenly dropped like an elevator, falling below the landing zone and into the trees as if we had lost power. I only had time to yell, "Hang on!" and pull pitch to cushion the landing. No one was hurt, and we had landed without turning over, but the aircraft was severely damaged, as we had fallen through a tree. I was staring through the windscreen at a huge tree right in front of my face. The engines were still running and I quickly shut them off to prevent a fire. What the hell had happened? Had we run into a downdraft? That couldn't be, because the wind was calm and the weather clear. Did we lose an engine? I didn't hear one shut down, and both were running when we got on the ground. At the time, I had no idea what caused the accident. Neither did my copilot or my flight mechanic.

The soldiers had been watching me approach for landing and observed the crash. They couldn't climb down to us because of the barbed wire surrounding the zone and possibly because land mines had been placed around it to prevent enemy encroachment, but they did notify the customer at LS-20A. Lloyd and Dave Kendall, his copilot, launched out of 20A in their Twin Pack and arrived overhead with intentions of hoisting us up. It was not a good idea, in my opinion. We were safe where we were, and this was something better done in daylight. I canvassed everybody, and we all agreed to wait. Lloyd landed at the outpost, picked up the wounded soldier, and departed for Udorn. We spent the night sitting on a log.

We tried to walk out of the forest to a clearing that would allow a rescue aircraft to land the next morning, but six hours after we started, our clothes had been literally torn off by the thorns in the dense brush, and we were still close enough to see the crash site. From the air the brush did not look as dense, but I could see why people had difficulty escaping and evading when I actually tried to walk through it. It was practically impenetrable. We were eventually able to get to a clearing, where John Fonburg, flying a Bell, picked us up and took us back to LS-20A.

Joe, the customer who had launched me the night before, took one look at my condition and loaned me a pair of his pants. They were way too short but better than what I had on, which were in tatters. We deadheaded back to Udorn in a C-123 and I caught a company bus to my house. I didn't have any keys to open the gate so had to yell to get Lucette to come out. She'd have had no way of knowing what had happened, and when she saw me at the gate—

scratched and bruised and obviously wearing someone else's pants—she didn't know whether to laugh or cry. I felt the same way.

Initially, the crash appeared to be pilot error. I couldn't explain it, but a tear down inspection revealed that one engine had been at full power and the other engine at flight idle when the crash occurred. Further investigation showed the torque control unit had erroneously sensed an over speed and shut down one engine when I needed it most. It happened to me a couple of other times afterward, but never at a critical time. I also learned that if it happened you could close the throttle and open it back up immediately and full power could be obtained. Perhaps, had I known, I may have been able to avoid the crash, but at night in elevated terrain and on final approach close to the ground and slowed to landing speed, I doubt if I would have had time to quickly close and open the throttle before hitting the ground. There was a lot of finger pointing and recriminations, but in the end I was returned to flight duty.

Night Train To Bangkok

Cell phones were not around in Laos or northern Thailand in the sixties and early seventies, and the Internet had not yet been invented. Even landlines were rare. All Air America flight crews were required to have radios in their houses, as communications between the base and the flight crews were handled either through radios or messages sent to the residence in a company Volkswagen bus, commonly called a B-bus.

In the residences, we all tried to find some resemblance of normalcy, because unlike armed forces personnel whose tour in a war zone usually lasted one year, Air America flight crews spent at least three years and many six to twelve years. The average military pilot flew five hundred hours a year, while Air America pilots averaged one thousand hours per year. Invariably, crewmen either had local girlfriends or brought their wives and children to Udorn or Vientiane to live. Often, girlfriends became wives, and many, if not most of these unions have lasted for years. The average salary then was anywhere between thirty and fifty thousand a year, depending on your position and the amount of hours you flew per year, but living with the local economy was expensive, unless you went totally native, and that was difficult for most employees. Wives and children simply couldn't, or wouldn't, in most cases.

Therefore, while the salary sounds high for that point in time, it really wasn't, and savings were miniscule at best. Many tried the stock market or other investments as ways to save for the unforeseeable future, given we came out alive, but most investment strategies were tenuous at best. Unless you were an expert, the stock market generated more losses than gains. Air America had a voluntary retirement plan, but most people did not participate, as, on average, the plan generated very little future income.

Some purchased property in the United States or another foreign country. I purchased an apartment in Spain for Lucette and the kids to go to, in case I bought the farm in Laos. ("Bought the farm" was a common phrase used by pilots to refer to an incident in which you crashed and died in a farmer's field, doing enough damage to cause the government to pay damages.) That property, too, was a shaky investment, however. I never could get a clear title on it. Years later, I was able to get one-half of my original investment back, and that was better than many others were seeing.

Air America arranged for very good schools for the children in both Udorn and Vientiane, with teachers who were highly qualified. Many of the students from those schools still communicate with each other and have lasting relationships.

The war effort, while it was happening, had a negative effect on family relationships, however. The pressure on families was tremendous. Wives never knew whether their husbands might be killed or grievously wounded, until the men showed up at home again after a week of being up-country in Laos. And for those whose husbands were killed in action, it was extremely hard. There was no closure; the family was just quickly packed up and deported to their home of record. The husband's salary was then stopped abruptly and the only income provided was from workmen's compensation, approximately two hundred fifty dollars a month, give or take, depending on how many dependents were in the family. Girlfriends, and even fiancés in more serious relationships that probably would culminate into marriage, received nothing and were left to grieve on their own, without even their friends to console them.

Air America bent FAA rules in other areas but still tried to adhere to the requirement that you had one day off for every six worked, and seven days off each month. After all, there was no way to communicate with your wife and children until you came home. In addition, combat flying was obviously strenuous, making it difficult to transition from war mode to father and husband mode all in one day. War was also addictive; even though the horror of it is repugnant, you found yourself wanting to get back into the action over and over again, making it hard to be with your family mentally, even when you were with them physically. I believe that addictiveness is due to the basic human desire to repulse evil and be a part of a project with a positive outcome. There is indescribable euphoria when acting to save lives and seeing a plan come together with a positive ending. You know that eventually it has to end, but deep inside, you really don't want it to.

A war that simply stops, with no victor and no tangible ending, has a negative impact on anyone who participates. It is severely depressing. But that's what happened in Laos. By the spring of 1974, the war was all but over there. The North Vietnamese were persecuting the Hmong, and the only desire of the Laotians was to be free to exist in the lifestyle that they had known for hundreds of years. In the end, not only had nothing been accomplished, but the life expectancy of a Hmong had decreased dramatically. We simply stopped and left them dangling in an ill wind, with no support and no answers to all of the questions about their plight.

I came to Udorn in 1969, and it now was the spring of 1974. I could have transferred to Saigon, but there was no place to school the kids and nothing for Lucette to do there, and the Twin Pack incident had taken the wind out of my sails. I could sense that the whole thing was over, but I couldn't quite escape the feeling that it wasn't yet time to leave. I decided to terminate my employment with Air America and began the process of moving out of Thailand. But still clinging to hope I may again be needed, I elected to remain in Southeast Asia and applied and was accepted for employment in Taiwan flying a civilian version of the Twin Pack. I was alerted to an opening with Great China Airlines who had a contract with Gulf Oil to carry personnel and supplies to an off-shore drill ship.

Last-minute details kept reminding me of past events, and memories flooded my mind. The furniture was packed and gone. Lucette and the kids had left a week before to go vacation in Spain. This was my last day in Udorn, and I would be leaving on the night train to Bangkok.

I was hot, sweaty, dirty, and tired, and only half-finished digging a large hole in the backyard. Old Dollar had been our family pet and watchdog that

Lucette and I acquired right after we married. We couldn't take him to Taipei, and we tried desperately to find him a home. But it wasn't easy to place a Great Dane who didn't like anyone outside of the immediate family. A local car dealership wanted him as a guard dog, but Dollar did not like any of the people there, and I knew his life would be miserable. The only alternative was to put him to sleep, and the family had left the task to me.

As it turned out, the local vet had not been able to get near enough to him to administer the lethal dose. Dollar would have none of that. So, I'd had to do it myself, while gently telling the big dog that everything would be okay. He had complete trust in me and died in my arms.

Now, I was in the process of burying him in the backyard—a perfectly good dog that wanted nothing more than to be left alone with his family. I felt terrible.

He required a big hole, and I rested often, leaning on the shovel while staring down at his lifeless body. I couldn't stop wondering why I felt like the bad guy when it was his disposition that had caused all of this. Then a memory flashed through my mind, and I laughed involuntarily. It hadn't been funny at the time, but it was funny now.

I often made homemade ice cream from strawberries I got from missionaries on the Boleven Plateau in the southern part of Laos when I worked at Pakse. I was in the process of finishing up a batch one day, when Charlie Basham, a fellow Air America pilot who lived in the same compound, walked into the house. Dollar raised his head, but Charlie didn't pay him any attention. Most dogs will not be bothered unless they sense danger, so I guess Dollar must have felt safe with him. Charlie had just gotten a big spoonful of ice cream into his mouth when our smaller dog barked for some reason. In the blink of an eye, Dollar was up and had his fangs sunk into Charlie's face.

Great Danes are not smart. I hope that doesn't offend anyone, but it's the truth. They react on instinct. Dollar sensed danger and reacted. Charlie never moved a muscle. He just looked that dog in the eye and continued chewing.

Not too many people can remain unmoving and stare a large dog in the eye while the animal's fangs are puncturing his face. I was stunned. So was the dog. The only one who was calm was Charlie.

Dollar backed off, whimpering, and Charlie finished off the ice cream.

"Charlie," I choked out. "I'll get my gun and shoot the damn dog right now!"

"Wait ten days," Charlie said.

"What?" I didn't know what he meant at first, and then realized ... rabies. Charlie wanted to make sure the dog didn't have rabies.

Charlie walked out, saying it was pretty good ice cream.

After ten days, Charlie told me not to shoot the dog. The fang marks had almost healed, and Charlie recognized that Lucette and the kids depended on Dollar for safety when I was up-country.

The memory helped me with the task at hand, and I kept on digging. Before long, I was out of breath and started thinking about the strawberries and the Boleven Plateau. Not long after arriving in Udorn, I had been designated as an instructor pilot in the H-34 program, both for new arrivals and for those transferring from Saigon. I was teamed up on this hitch in Pakse with Link Luckett. Link had been in Saigon flying the Bell and was actually senior to me. In fact, Link was more than just senior to me; he had probably forgotten more about helicopter flying than I had ever learned. One of his accomplishments was the rescue of some mountain climbers near the eighteen-thousand-foot level of Mount McKinley, with a normally aspirated helicopter. No small feat. He was awarded the Carnegie Silver Medal for that heroic effort.

He also received the Frederick L. Feinberg Award in 1961. This award was presented to the helicopter pilot(s) who accomplished the most outstanding achievement during the preceding calendar year, and honored the memory of an outstanding helicopter test pilot, and an exemplary person. The award consisted of a stipend of two hundred dollars, the engraving of the recipient's name on a plaque, and an individual plaque.

Well, here I was showing this award-winning helicopter pilot how to fly an H-34, which was redundant. However, like most good pilots, Link was also a good student. We were working out of PS-22, supplying food, water, and hard rice (a code word used by the company to mean ammunition, which we were not supposed to be carrying) to the several outposts on the Plateau. We heard on the guard channel that an A-7 Corsair had been shot down just off the Plateau. The single pilot involved was in the process of escaping and evading some highly pissed-off people, whom he had been bombing the crap out of before they knocked him down. Two A-1 Skyraiders were discussing the situation, and I asked if we could assist.

They told me that they were waiting for a Jolly Green rescue helicopter coming from Vietnam but asked if we could stick around in case they needed something done right away.

I asked for the location, and when they told me, I knew that the pilot's survival depended on moving him immediately. He was in a bad place and would not be well-liked.

"Hey," I said. "Either get him out now or there won't be anything to get."

They agreed.

In the air, a few miles from the spot where the man was thought to be hiding, we came into contact with the pilot on the ground, and he reported activity all around him.

I intended to make a high-speed descent to tree level, instruct him to ignite the smoke grenade that was normally carried in a pilot's survival vest and make a fast stop right over his head. We couldn't land—there were too many trees. So we would have to hoist him up. I explained to him how we were going to do it, and then I asked the two Skyraiders if they would strafe the areas to either side of me as I picked him up and as we departed.

They agreed, and down we went, with the Skyraiders right alongside my aircraft. I was using a high-speed autorotation descent and halfway down I called for smoke. It was red and billowing in the trees, and I knew that if I could see it, the bad guys could too.

We were in the tree line now and moving as fast as an H-34 can go at about 120 knots. Sitting in a helicopter with 1,525 horsepower roaring in your ear, ground fire sounds like popcorn cooking in the next room. I could hear the popcorn now, and it was popping fast and heavy.

The Skyraiders were unleashing everything they had and jabbering loudly to each other over the radio. I should have placed them on another frequency, but I wanted to keep contact with both them and the downed pilot.

"Hold it down, guys!" I yelled. "I can't hear the survivor."

"Okay, Mister. Do your thing," they yelled back.

I was over the smoke now, and I did a high-speed stop right on the mark, but I couldn't see the pilot. I turned in a hover looking for him, and Link was calmly telling me to keep it into the wind. The flight mechanic was busy dropping the hoist when I spotted our man. I stopped dead still in a hover so the pilot could get into the hoist.

I could hear the popcorn going like crazy, and I had my wheels in the trees, trying to get as low as I could and hoping like hell I didn't catch a tail rotor. Link was scanning the area looking for bad guys, and we both knew our time was limited.

"Tell me when he's aboard," I yelled to the flight mechanic. "We gotta get out of here."

"He's on board. Haul ass!"

I moved out of the hover while keeping the wheels in the trees, with fifty inches of manifold pressure and the turns pulled down to 2,650 for best lift over drag—a trick that either Ed Rudolph or John Fonburg (both former Marines and former Air America pilots) taught me. The bad guys knew we had grabbed their mark, and they were pouring on the firepower. The two Skyraiders were dropping everything they had alongside us, and the black smoke from the spent ordnance was heavy.

Wham!

"We're hit!" I yelled. We couldn't stay down at tree level. Our only choice was to climb out of trouble. I had been hit before, but this sounded like big stuff. It had really rocked the helicopter.

The problem was, although the H-34 descended quickly, its climb was painfully slow. And it seemed especially slow when someone was shooting at you.

I yelled, "Climb, you son of a bitch!" I was looking for a cloud to hide in, and the Skyraiders were making pass after pass to hold the enemies' heads down. I felt like my butt was pinching holes in the seat cushion as I pulled up on the control stick, trying to urge the aircraft up faster. Of course, it was no benefit whatsoever.

And then we were clear. I checked below and everybody was okay. We headed back to PS-22 in silence, escorted by the Skyraiders. Without them, we could not have made it.

Dutch, the CIA case officer for the Pakse site we were operating from met us at the helicopter when we landed. We asked the pilot where he was from, and he spouted off his name, rank, and serial number. We all laughed. Soldiers who are captured in battle are instructed to only give their name, rank, and serial number when questioned. I guess our civilian clothes were confusing to him, and I assured him we were not the enemy. I never understood the rationale for keeping Air America's presence in Laos a secret from military pilots who operated in harm's way in the exact area we were located. The best chance for survival when shot down is a quick extraction. Was it military jealousy? All the A-7 pilot had to do was tell us he was coming in the area and to listen up in case something went wrong. In this case he was rescued, but for many others their plight was capture and death.

The heat brought me back to reality. I was only halfway through digging the hole.

"Damn it, Dollar! Why couldn't you have been a cat?"

It was late, and I needed to finish. I kept looking out into the compound, hoping to see a B-bus with a note telling me things weren't really over, and to saddle up and head north.

I finished covering up the grave and stood silently. Then I went back to the house, washed up, and left, locking the front door for the last time. I went to the Charoen Hotel for a quiet dinner, and then a taxi took me to the train station.

I kept telling myself that I shouldn't be depressed and that the lifestyle all of us lived was not conducive to longevity. I had been flying in a combat zone almost continually since 1964. Wasn't it time just to accept that this war was over? But where were the accolades, the victory parades and back slaps?

"Get over it, man!" I kept telling myself. "It's done and finished ... okay ... I accept it." But just as I boarded the train, I thought I heard a VW engine. I rushed outside. Was it B-bus? No, I was mistaken. I dejectedly climbed back on board.

The train slowly pulled out of the station and headed south to Bangkok. I kept thinking that someone would get in touch and tell me to go back. But no one ever did—and deep down inside, I could feel myself fighting with the realization that it really was over.

The Last Day

The war in Southeast Asia ended for American GIs in 1972, but it didn't end for Air America until April 29, 1975. I interviewed several of the pilots about their experiences on that last day while conducting research for an application to seek veteran status for former Air America employees. It was a grim ending.

When the war in Laos ended, Air America employees scattered like leaves in the wind. Some transferred to Saigon, where the flying had always been routine compared to the paramilitary work in Laos. It was still dangerous, but business as usual would not continue. Most of the military had long gone and the South Vietnamese now were controlling their own destiny.

Nixon had resigned. He had done what he'd promised and ended America's military involvement in Vietnam, but his resignation in the face of impeachment sapped his energy, and Vietnam was floundering and essentially rudderless. Ford was still trying to find his way and running out of time to do it. The speed and determination the North Vietnamese army was using to overrun South Vietnam in 1975 was surprising and unexpected by the Ford Administration. The truth was the situation was hopeless. An era spanning thirty years was coming to an end, but denial seemed to be the popular word. Gobs of information from the left and the right about America's Vietnam policy was spewing from every corner, but the rhetoric did nothing for those whose life and property in the region was now in jeopardy. The end result was that people acted with instinct and goodness of heart, because all of the hastily crafted plans were evaporating before they could be implemented.

During the height of the Vietnam War, the streets of Saigon had been filled with American military vehicles and soldiers. But now, almost all of the American troops had departed. It was obvious to everyone, except possibly the American Embassy, that Saigon would fall. Buon Me Thuot had been overrun in March. Da Nang had fallen soon after, and then Nha Trang. Yet for some reason, the American ambassador believed that Saigon would be spared to remain a neutral enclave. The ambassador did not want to enact a full-scale evacuation for fear it would give the wrong signal to the encroaching North Vietnamese and hinder his negotiating position. He was under intense pressure with encouragement from one side and censure on the other. The truth was he didn't have a choice. The North Vietnamese were coming, and they were not in the mood to negotiate.

The American Embassy had received word that Americans and Vietnamese who supported them had been executed when the North Vietnamese overran cities in the north. Evacuating Americans was of course paramount, but equally important was evacuating those Vietnamese who actively supported American interests, and who could very well be killed if Saigon fell. How to accomplish this monumental task without capitulation or even with complete surrender was the conundrum.

Civilian organizations that answered to their company's board of directors departed with what equipment they could hurriedly gather up. Air America remained because Air America answered to the president of the United States, and they would leave when he said so.

Air America's management conducted meetings with embassy officials over several days determining radio frequencies and locations of ships off the coast, and to establish a contingency plan. Air America's initial plan was to evacuate indigenous Air America employees. There were thirty-two designated helicopter pickup points on various buildings in Saigon. Six were assigned to Air America. Ralph Begian worked in Air America's Flight Information Center. He and Nikki Fillippi, an Air America helicopter pilot, worked relentlessly to prepare pickup points in the city. But the American ambassador, his staff, and the Vietnamese police thwarted their plans to provide refueling points. The explanation received from the ambassador was that overt plans of this nature might cause panic among the local Vietnamese population. Air America's management did their best to improvise and moved to a single building to maintain communications.

US Marine Corps General Carey told Air America representatives that Marines were supposed to be stationed at the Air America complex to protect the fuel depots at least six hours prior to any evacuation, but said that his hands were tied as the ambassador had refused to give approval until well into the afternoon. That meant the Marines didn't show up, and the closest fuel was on the ships off the coast, a full eighty to a hundred miles from Saigon. Consequently, fuel would prove to be a big problem on the last day, and all of the carefully laid plans would have to be scrapped.

On April 28, ground fire from unknown sources shot down several aircraft over Saigon. The next day, Air America's fixed-wing group rescued what refugees they could from the area and departed for Bangkok, Thailand. The next day rockets and artillery fire from the North Vietnamese Army severely damaged Saigon's Tan Son Nhut airport. The ambassador, making a personal observation, declared the airport unsafe for fixed wing and ordered all evacuations would be by helicopter only. Air America's helicopter crews were ordered to remain to aid in the evacuation. Thus, in a rush, the Saigon exodus began. The largest refugee airlift of the entire war was about to unfold.

CIA Contract employee O. B. Harnage reaches out of an Air America helicopter to pull up evacuees during the evacuation of Saigon. Photo used under license by Corbis.

One of the Air America pickup points was the Pittman Building in downtown Saigon, where Dutch photojournalist Hugh van Es shot his famous photograph of refugees climbing the ladder to reach the helicopter. When you look at this historic image, you can't help but focus on the man reaching his arm out to help.

The photo shown here is not the Hugh van Es shot but was taken at almost exactly the same time, from a different angle. This particular image clearly shows the Air America markings on the tail of the helicopter. Despite the difference in angle, you can easily see the man at the top of the ladder, reaching out to help the evacuees.

No one knows for sure who the helicopter crew was. They didn't know they were being photographed, nor would they have cared. For years, throughout Southeast Asia, they'd been hauling in food, ammunition, water, and fresh troops, and hauling out wounded. Thus, this photo is a snapshot in time—a glimpse that epitomizes the essence of what Air America was all about.

The man holding out his hand in the photo was a CIA contract employee named O. B. Harnage, who, after the fall of Saigon, told me in a personal interview, "We kept telling them we would come back. And then we didn't."

Harnage is now deceased, but his words live on in those of us who were there. In fact, I think that's what bothered most of us who worked in Southeast Asia all those years. We never went back. We never had closure.

Air America's several hundred Filipino employees were last on the list to get out of the city, and those with Vietnamese families were especially vulnerable.

As with the Koreans in Nha Trang, the Philippine government stationed a ship off the coast of Saigon to receive the Filipino evacuees, but the Vietnamese police would not let them board. As a result, more than a thousand Filipino personnel were stranded on the beach.

Marius Burke, an Air America helicopter pilot, was then able to convince Filipino Minister of Affairs to let him bypass the dock and airlift the evacuees to the ship. They were able to evacuate more than six hundred people this way. The other four hundred were evacuated by barge during the night.

Air America tried to get its Vietnamese employees onto the same ship, requesting assistance from the US embassy. There was plenty of room, and the Filipino Minister of Affairs gave his blessing, but the US embassy said no. They were afraid that South Vietnamese soldiers would sneak aboard and mix in among the Vietnamese evacuees, and the thinking was they were needed to defend Saigon. Because the embassy refused to cooperate, many of Air America's Vietnamese employees were left behind.

During the evacuation, tragedies were as common as boards on a picket fence, but spontaneous acts of heroism occurred just as often.

On one occasion, Ralph Begian ended up hanging out of his helicopter without a safety strap to pull a Vietnamese man aboard. Unheralded and unknown, Ralph risked his own life repeatedly, performing acts of heroism for no other reason than it was the right thing to do.

In another instance, Nikki Fillippi, along with Ed Reid, another Air America helicopter pilot veteran, maintained a communication post throughout the day. They had to move the post twice, due to enemy activity, and finally evacuated to the USS *Hancock* that evening.

Outlying ships were supposed to have known about Air America's role in the evacuation, but there had been an obvious communication gap, which created one particularly hairy emergency situation.

Many South Vietnamese helicopters headed out to sea, hoping to land on one of the ships and escape the North Vietnamese. However, groups of aircraft with no advanced warning and no radio communications were all trying to land at once. They paid no attention to standard flight patterns or landing protocol. Dangerous was not even the word for it.

In response, the commander of the USS *Blue Ridge* took extreme measures to protect his ship and crew. He ordered the helicopter pilots to land with their passengers, but then to take off and ditch the aircraft at sea. He arranged for a small boat standing by to pick them up when they surfaced. He demanded the same for Air America crews, not realizing that they were part of the planned evacuation effort and would simply be landing to off load their passengers and refuel for the next trip.

Ditching at sea is an emergency maneuver, and it's dangerous. There's no way to do it safely or gracefully. The procedure called for the removal of the helicopter doors, to give the pilot a reasonable chance of escaping the sinking aircraft.

Chauncey Collard was then fifty-five and had piloted every aircraft the U.S. Navy had owned since 1936. Chauncey had been an Air America helicopter pilot for several years, but he was about to experience an entirely new kind of adventure. As soon as he landed aboard the *Blue Ridge*, the ship's crew removed his doors and ordered him to take off and ditch his aircraft. It didn't seem like a good idea to Chauncey, so he headed back to Saigon for another load of evacuees, stopping first to refuel at a ship that was more lenient.

He told me years later that he remembered it being a little breezy, flying the rest of the day without doors. For the several people who remembered how Chauncey had saved them, his decision to continue was a godsend. He didn't have to do it. Orders or not, this was beyond any justifiable requirement. He could have very well refused and gone below in the ship and safety.

The decision of the USS *Blue Ridge* also endangered Air America pilot Dave Kendall. Dave and Ruth Kendall and their kids, Bobby and Vicky, were well known in Air America. Originally from Hornbeak, Tennessee, Dave had started with the company in Saigon, transferred to Laos for several years, and was now back in Saigon. He had two brightly colored shirts that he alternately wore with bib overalls whenever he wasn't flying.

Flying out of uniform was strictly forbidden, but Dave figured this last day was an exception and the overalls seemed more comfortable. When he landed aboard the USS *Blue Ridge* with refugees, the ship's crew took one look at his outfit, determined he must have stolen the helicopter and ordered him to ditch his aircraft.

The recommended procedure for ditching is to land in the water and turn the helicopter on its side, while the blades are still turning. Dave decided to do it differently. He trimmed the aircraft nose down about twenty feet above the water and jumped out.

When he jumped out, the helicopter's center of gravity shifted, and the blades almost hit him. The sailors scooped him out of the water, and sent him below deck, where he changed shirts but kept his overalls. This video clearly shows Air America's involvement and David jumping out of his helicopter.[7]

By this time the *Blue Ridge* was able to halfway sort out the rogue helicopters fleeing Saigon from the Air America helicopters carrying refugees. Air America helicopter pilot Larry Stadulis was also told to stand down at the ship, and he too was sent below. A short time later, he was told he was needed to go back to fly an unattended helicopter. Dave Kendall, seeing that Larry was going back, climbed in with him. They shuttled back and forth between ship and shore, hauling in refugees the rest of the day.

By nightfall, both men were mentally and physically exhausted, as they found themselves in the middle of the South China Sea, in light rain, trying to find the carrier USS *Midway.* All light aboard the *Midway* had been extinguished, however, as the situation had required the U.S. Navy to create a blackout; this made the ship nearly impossible to detect. To make matters worse, the twenty-minute low-fuel light in the helicopter had been on for fifteen minutes, and no one actually knew how accurate those lights were.

Larry and Dave were in trouble. They were calling for help from the *Midway*, and the ship's radar could see them, but they couldn't see the ship. The low-fuel warning light kept getting brighter and brighter. To boot, throughout the day, it had been obvious that Air America's key role in the evacuation was not clearly understood by the other players, as cooperation from those who were supposed to be informed had been slim to none. The ship also was not sure who was in the helicopter. In this situation, however, the *Midway's* cooperation was imperative.

Larry informed the *Midway* that they could not see the ship and needed a light. It was now time for the *Midway's* commanding officer to make up his mind and do it fast.

The helicopter had only a few minutes of fuel remaining when the *Midway* relented and turned on every topside light. Larry said it looked like a Christmas tree, and it was most definitely a gift. Larry and Dave landed on the flight deck, running on nothing more than fumes.

The *Blue Ridge* sailed to Hong Kong and unceremoniously dropped the Air America crews. Air America management gathered them together and

7 http://www.youtube.com/watch?v=mcQoQDkhbYw&feature=related

simply told them to go home, or whereever they wanted. It was over. No fare-thee-well and no closing. It stopped abruptly without explanation.

More than thirty Air America flight crews stayed and flew the last day. It would be difficult to justify the carnage that took place in that war. But Air America didn't start that war, and neither did the other soldiers who fought there. Nor did we perpetuate it. Right, wrong, or indifferent, we did our job and often performed duties above and beyond those assigned to us.

Though Air America was noncombatant and our work humanitarian, we were still soldiers. Joe Galloway, coauthor of *We Were Soldiers Once … and Young*, perhaps said it best when he wrote, "We Were Soldiers: That's the way it is; that's what we were. We put it simply, without swagger, without brag, in those three plain words. We speak them softly, just *to* ourselves, just *for* ourselves. If you can't hear those echoes, you weren't; if you can, you were."

Were our efforts worth it? Some writers have said that the picture of the helicopter on the Pittman building signified America's failed policy. Echoing that opinion, many have stated that they feel that those who risked their lives to save others did so only as a part of a strong work ethic, with no thought at all toward the plight of our fellow men. Conversely, others feel that all of us share a social responsibility; they feel that values such as integrity and kindness are what make America great, and that such values come into sharpest focus when they are least expected. I take the latter view. After all, life is not always fair, but that does not mean we should abandon hope and leave favorable consequences only to those who are clever.

I have often been asked why I joined Air America, and then why I stayed. I could quote many very good writers who have tried to explain why some men volunteer to go to war, but I'm not sure they got it right either. So let's look at the current events for a minute, and I'll see if I can present a rational answer.

People have told me that they voted for Obama because they thought he would get America out of Iraq and Afghanistan. These same people also frequently say that they champion peace and are firmly against war, with all its evil and horror—and that they were against Bush because he led us to war.

Yet a strong American majority cheered on Obama when he sent the SEAL team to kill Osama Bin Laden. Wasn't that war? They also cheered when he sent in the Navy to capture the pirates who commandeered the commercial ship off the coast of Somalia. Was that not war as well? How would the public have responded had either of those missions failed? And why do the American Legion and the Veterans of Foreign Wars celebrate war, if they are against it?

I believe Americans are against the *uncertainties* of war, and against failure specifically, and that it is for these reasons they would like to forget Vietnam and Korea—because there was no official end to either.

Think about it. Bush was very popular initially, when Saddam was ousted, but thereafter, as the war languished, people said they were against it. Really, I think Bush would have been a hero had there been a positive ending.

I also don't believe that people who say they're against war are just against violence. Even the most vehement protesters to the war in Vietnam were violent in their own responses. And now I'm told that the majority of Americans favor water boarding, after the method was effective at capturing and killing bin Laden.

On the other hand, people who justify war do so for altruistic reasons.

For these reasons, I feel I can safely say that all of us are warlike in one fashion or another, and that our varied responses to it simply depend on how the war is structured, described, and delivered. War, in its pure state, is the crucible that melds men and aspires them to greatness. Who can forget John Wayne, for example? Who among us would not step forward with fists to right a wrongful act?

Yet war is never entirely pure. It has been said there is a war for every reason and a reason for every war, although we often don't like to analyze the reasons too carefully because people on both sides can justify their actions. When at war with America, the Japanese, Germans, North Vietnamese, and North Koreans all considered themselves freedom fighters against American imperialists. Perhaps the Bible offers the best lesson in how war can be twisted; one only needs to look at David, who sent the husband of the woman he desired into battle so he could have his way with her.

Perhaps Taylor Caldwell offered an explanation in her book *The Captains and the Kings* when she said that all wars are fought for bullets, meaning sales of war materials is the impetus for such action. There is a certain amount of truth in that statement, but I don't believe war is conducted solely for financial gain. At the same time, you couldn't stop the war in the Middle East abruptly without putting the hundreds of thousands of Americans employed making war materials out of work. Understanding this concept is difficult because of the diversity in cultures. How a person thinks on a ranch in Montana cannot be equated with those who dwell in New York City.

There is a good chance we will always be at war. To appease the public we just keep changing the reasons for doing so.

Looking back, the time I spent in combat was the best time of my life. It was almost tangible, the feeling of, first, being tested and, second, overcoming the adversity. Yet in many respects it was hideous and heart wrenching. What part was the best? Doing it right. What part was hideous? Seeing the aftermath when it had been done wrong.

I never got any enjoyment killing people, but doing medical evacuations under fire and rescuing downed aircrew members was euphoric, and as such, while others may differ, I believe that combat operations with a positive outcome can be addictive. The emphasis should be placed on the positive outcome. Positive outcome is the same reason all presidents are cheered for war-like actions coupled with success and rebuked for war that ends in failure.

For me, then, going back to war meant going back into a difficult environment, where I could be tested and succeed. I was looking at war from a pure, untainted standpoint, and I was looking forward to a positive outcome. I don't think psychic income can be measured, but I believe this is the same reason why men and women everywhere perform any endeavor. Air America seemed like a good place to accomplish this goal of success, because, at the time, it didn't look like I was ever going to get back to Vietnam with the Marines.

The Truth About Air America And The CIA

It took several years of research to understand what Air America was about. All of the roads I followed from my personal experiences and exhaustive research pointed in different directions and to various conclusions.

I believe you need to understand Air America's roots to better explain its mission. Air America began as an ongoing operation that became a series of projects, which, over a period of twenty-five years, went through progressive elaboration and change. Essentially, it started because the US government needed military presence in areas where the US military could not go, due to public pressure and treaty constraints.

The initial ongoing operation was CNRRA Air Transport, a Chinese company owned by General Claire Chennault and Whiting Willauer with a Chinese bank as an investor and part owner. CNRRA eventually became Civil Air Transport and was generally called CAT. The airline was one of three operating in China and the smallest of the lot. Willauer had wanderlust and a desire for adventure. He was highly educated, a Princeton graduate and Harvard attorney, and served with honor in a number of government jobs. What was happening in China and the threat of Communism garnered much of his attention.

Under the lend-lease program initiated by Roosevelt, Willauer secured a position with China Defense Supplies. Prior to the outbreak of WW II, Willauer helped organize the American volunteer group that most people know as the Flying Tigers. Willauer was enthralled with war and with the sense of purpose that came with being involved, an attitude that I can identify with. He desperately wanted to succeed with his airline, and succeed he did, until civil war broke out between the Nationalists and the Communists.

Prior to hostilities, CAT had hauled freight consisting of live animals, furs, tin, cotton, and a variety of other materials mostly for relief efforts in inland China, but when the civil war broke out, CAT started hauling troops, munitions, wounded, and all of the other supplies necessary to conduct a war.

When the Nationalists lost, CAT helped move Chiang Kai-Shek, the Nationalist leader, to Formosa. And with that, CAT's tenure in Mainland China was over, leaving them in serious financial trouble.

Thereafter, Chennault and Willauer went to the US State Department with the argument that Communism could easily, and quickly, spread south along the Pacific Rim and eventually threaten America. They wanted the US government to fund the airline so they could continue to damper Communist expansion with clandestine activity in and around China, but the State Department was not interested in direct ownership of a Chinese company and turned a cold shoulder.

The newly formed CIA, however, was a champion for the company's assets and position in Southeast Asia, as the agency had found good use in the airline for clandestine intelligence gathering. So, the CIA devised an elaborate plan wherein the airline could be purchased *indirectly,* and State consented.

Saying the CIA purchased and owned CAT, therefore, is not correct. The CIA does not have any money; it is funded by the Department of Defense. The CIA also does not have a foreign policy; the US government has a foreign policy and uses the CIA as a tool for administering that policy. Consequently, the CIA could technically operate the company but could never own it.

The result: a Delaware corporation was formed by the name of Airdale, which formed a subsidiary by the name of CAT, Inc. CAT, Inc. purchased 40 percent of Civil Air Transport, and 60 percent remained with Chinese investors. All of the CAT pilots were transferred to CAT, Inc. CAT, Inc., in turn, opened a company called Asiatic Aeronautical Company, LTD, and it was this company that owned and leased all of the aircraft operated by CAT,

Inc. and Civil Air Transport. Asiatic Aeronautical Company, LTD, was also the maintenance facility for the company, and, over the years, expanded into a huge aircraft-maintenance company capable of building a complete aircraft from the ground up.

It was a convoluted organization with comingling of funds and hidden directives. Almost immediately, the CIA, who was charged with operating the company, was overwhelmed by the staggering cost.

By 1949, CAT had more than eight hundred employees and forty-some aircraft. The airline was in danger of failure, and the CIA did not have enough work to keep it afloat. So it was decided to expand the company's role and allow it to bid for lucrative government contracts.

Some airline companies, such as Northwest, who knew about CAT's true ownership, realized that CAT, Inc. was in effect contracting itself and paying itself back, which gave it an unfair advantage. They threatened to publicly expose the airline, which caused a flurry of diplomatic activity, but ultimately kept quiet, allowing CAT, Inc. to bid along with other airlines. I am not completely sure why Northwest Air agreed to cooperate, because their complaint was valid, but I do know that governments have ways of swaying opinions. For example, one very large company asked me once, when I complained about a breach of contract, "Just how much money are you willing to spend for justice?" I'm not saying that was the case with Northwest Air, but, regardless, the issue was settled.

The first CAT, Inc. contract was for Operation Booklift in Korea, and it was not a CIA operation. Jesse Walton, a former CAT/Air America employee I talked about earlier, brought a book to my attention by Captain A. G. Thompson, which describes all of CAT's contract operations extensively.[8] The information about CAT is contained in a single chapter. The second paragraph of Chapter 48 explicitly discusses the CAT/US military connection: "CAT, Incorporated was formed in 1950 for the specific purpose of providing commercial airlift for US military and government agencies in the Far East." The information given by Thompson here is not exactly true. As mentioned,

---

8 Captain A. G. Thompson, *The Greatest Airlift, The Story of Combat Cargo,* printed by Dai-Nippon Printing Company, Tokyo, Japan, May 1954, Chapter 48, page 449

originally, the company was specifically formed for CIA clandestine activity, but the CIA could not justify the enormous expense, and needed outside work to keep the company solvent. In fact, most of the work conducted by CAT/ Air America was through government contracts or executive-department requirements that had nothing to do with the CIA. The point is, however, that Thompson acknowledged a relationship between CAT and the US military, and it was this nexus that provided collaboration for my request for veteran status.

Further down the page, Thompson wrote,

> Missions were assigned to CAT in the early days just as to any military squadron. The pilot was directed to fly from Tachikawa to Pusan with a load of cargo, pick up a load of wounded and fly them to Itazuke, fly deadhead (empty) to Ashiya and pick up a load of ammo, fly to Taegu and pick up another load of wounded, and so on until the mission was finally concluded, sometimes several days later. Combat Cargo flight nurses and medics traveled with the CAT planes just as they did on the military planes.

The last paragraph in Chapter 48 of Thompson's book provides a vivid description of the sacrifices that CAT/Air America pilots began making in 1950, which continued until 1975. Thompson wrote,

> Five members of the CAT Incorporated flying staff gave their lives on the Korean Airlift. Although civilians, the pilots took all the risks of the military members of the Combat Cargo operation, including the possibility of making the ultimate sacrifice. The CAT on the Airlift had done a good job.

Were they civilians? Not really. In 1954, the French Republic contracted CAT to assist them with their war effort against the Vietminh; this also was not a CIA project. The French had first requested the assistance of the American government, but Eisenhower had been too embroiled in the 1954

Geneva Convention to become actively involved with deploying US military personnel.

A scheme was thus developed in which CAT pilots would operate USAF C-119 aircraft from Clark Air Force Base in the Philippines. The aircraft would be painted in French Republic colors. CAT made numerous airdrops into the besieged French Republic garrison at Dien Bien Phu using these aircraft. Several aircrew members were wounded and one aircraft was shot down, killing the pilot, James B. McGovern Jr., and copilot Wallace Buford. They may have been the first casualties of the Vietnam War.

The US government never recognized their effort and sacrifice. Fifty years later, in a ceremony at the home of the ambassador of France in Washington DC, the French government honored those still living with the Legion of Honor, which is France's highest military civilian honor.

The gesture by the French was most certainly appreciated, even though fifty years late, but where was the recognition from the US government? Where is it today? Inconceivably, to me, the DNI report requested by Congress points to the honor bestowed on Air America pilots, as if the CIA had something to do with it, but fails to mention that the US government, to this day, refuses to even discuss it.

However in the late fifties, CAT pilots operated B-26 combat aircraft from Clark in a battle against Communist forces in Indonesia, which was a CIA project—but it should be understood that the CIA does not perform this kind of work without approval of the Department of State and the Department of Defense.

In this battle, one pilot, Alan Pope, was shot down, captured, sentenced to death, and later repatriated through diplomatic efforts by the Kennedy administration. His wingman, Connie Segrist, who flew many, many covert flights in a variety of aircraft, retired on just social security, to my best knowledge, and made ends meet working in a Home Depot store in California.

Connie recently passed away, but prior to his death, I talked to him several times—once at one of the CAT reunions and a couple of times by phone when I was seeking information. He loved to spend time providing funny anecdotal accounts about his experiences but never talked about secret activity. Connie may have actually worked for the CIA, but if so, he was a contract employee and I don't believe ever received any retirement benefits. Maybe I'm wrong, however; I can only hope he received what he deserved.

Connie, along with Douglas Price, another CAT employee, was also involved with the Fulton Sky Hook operation, flying a B-17. The mission was successful due to the dedication and expertise of these two pilots and their crew.[9] Should that address not be accessible, seek information from any server, using the key words "Robert Fulton's Skyhook" and "Operation Coldfeet." I often wondered whether the people that Connie assisted knew what the man had accomplished.

Connie was married to Nora Sun. The marriage ended in divorce, but they had three sons. Nora's grandfather was Sun Yat Sen. In Chinese history he is known as "The Father of the Revolution" or "The Father of the Republic." In the West, he is considered the most important figure of Chinese history in the twentieth century.

Nora and her mother had fled to Hong Kong when Mao's troops seized the family's villa. After graduating from high school, Nora became the youngest flight attendant for Civil Air Transport, where she met Connie. Sadly, Nora was recently killed in an auto accident in Taiwan. I did not know her well but found her to be a very pleasant woman when we talked at reunions. One of their sons was present at the dependents' reunion, at which I unveiled the H-34 painting.

In 1957, Airdale changed its name to The Pacific Corporation. Then in 1959, CAT, Inc. changed its name to Air America, Inc., after two years of objections by Air France. Asiatic Aeronautical's name was changed in 1959 to Air Asia Company, LTD.

In the early sixties, Kennedy, like Eisenhower had, could see Communist expansion in Laos, a landlocked country considered the lynchpin to continued encroachment throughout the Pacific Rim. Kennedy saw that military presence in Laos was a requirement but couldn't justify the continued presence of the US military.

Air America was the logical choice. And when the Geneva Accords were

---

9 https://www.cia.gov/library/center-for-the-study-of-intelligence/csi-publications/csi-studies/studies/95unclass/Leary.html

signed in 1962, preventing US military presence in Laos, Air America became the only option.

Getting around in Laos was difficult. Air was practically the only solution, but airplanes alone could not handle the logistics. The Bell 47 bubble-canopy helicopter and the HO4S Chickasaw were introduced, but the Bell could not carry cargo and the HO4S didn't have the power to operate in the mountains.

Kennedy thus ordered the Marines to turn over several of the H-34 helicopters in their arsenal to Air America. Several Marine Corps pilots stationed in Okinawa were released from active service and employed by Air America to operate them.

Operations in the early sixties were light and all for the CIA, but in 1964, the Pathet Lao shot down a U.S. Navy F-8 Crusader photo aircraft and the pilot was captured. The navy went ballistic and demanded armed escorts for the photo flights, as well as SAR protection.

Air America did not enjoy the same concern. When an Air America C-46 was shot down in 1963, the government never bothered to seek rescue or release. The pilot and copilot were killed, but the kickers parachuted to safety and were captured and held captive. One, a Thai by the name of Pisidhi, escaped and went back to work with Air America, and his description of his ordeal was horrifying. He observed the aircraft blowing up with the pilot and copilot still aboard. (You can read his story, which also appeared in *Smoke Jumpers* magazine, on the Air America Association website.[10]) Another of the kickers, an American named Gene DeBruin, escaped but was recaptured and presumed dead.

Dieter Dengler, a U.S. Navy pilot, was also imprisoned with them and escaped. A movie titled *Rescue Dawn* told the Dengler story but portrayed DeBruin unfavorably. Both Dengler and Pisidhi said that DeBruin's portrayal was false. They said that DeBruin died trying to escape with his fellow kicker, Y. C., whom he refused to leave by himself, but who had malaria and was therefore too weak to escape. Clearly, Air America crewmembers were on their own in Laos.

10 http://air-america.org/Articles/Phisit.shtml)

Curtiss-Wright C-46. Photo used by permission of Tom Lum.

Military aircrew members shot down over Laos could not depend on military SAR assistance, because the 1962 Geneva Convention forbid them to be in Laos. Thailand and Vietnam were simply too far away. The solution was to designate Air America as primary SAR for Northern Laos, and the secretary of state did this in writing.[11] Additional H-34 helicopters were ordered to Air America precisely for this effort. Later, in the late sixties and early seventies, Air America became secondary SAR but was still involved in several SAR situations.

Military armed escort logistics for downed aircraft was also a problem. After a lot of wrangling, select Air America pilots were quickly trained in the T-28 that had been configured with armament and, for two years, conducted combat operations in Laos. Although this operation, called Operation Water Pump, was hotly debated, the president, the ambassador to Laos, and the Defense and State departments made the final decisions. It had nothing whatsoever to do with the CIA.

A series of USAF contracts were issued to Air America, along with contracts from the United States Agency for International Development (USAID). In Vietnam, Air America operated mostly to fulfill USAID and

11 http://www.utdallas.edu/library/collections/speccoll/Leeker/history/Laos3.pdf

Civil Operations and Rural Development Support (CORDS) contracts, but had USAF contracts as well. Air America, to my knowledge, had nothing to do with operations carried out by USAID or CORDS, and simply furnished transportation to move personnel to various locations at their request. As far as we were concerned they were the clients, yet the truth was the United States government owned us all. The difference was, the clients received government benefits, which included health care and retirement, and we didn't.

One USAF contract in Laos designated Air America as joint SAR with the USAF for Site 85, the ultra secret radar station in northern Laos. When Site 85 was overrun in 1968 it was two Air America choppers who picked up the only survivors and did so under fire. One survivor was killed after being shot while inside the helicopter.

All of the military personnel received decorations, including the Medal of Honor. In a UPI photograph of the event by Roger L. Wollenberg, as President Obama hands the medal to one of Master Sergeant Etchberger's sons standing in, you can clearly see both of their eyes on the white-haired man sitting in front. That man was Air America Captain Ken Wood. He and Flight Mechanic Rusty Irons were invited to the ceremony but were not publicly recognized. [12]

The North Vietnamese, using old biplanes configured to carry bombs, attacked Site 85 a couple months before the fall. Flying in the vicinity, Air America helicopter pilot, Captain Ted Moore observed the action and flew alongside, allowing the flight mechanic, Glen Woods, to shoot one down with an AK-47 assault rifle he carried for survival in case of a forced landing. This is the only recorded case of a helicopter shooting down a fixed-wing aircraft in any war.

In 1969, Nixon vowed to end the war in Vietnam after he was elected. He used two techniques to deliver on his promise. First, he and Dr. Henry Kissinger secretly made an agreement with China to force Taiwan off the United Nations Security Council and place the People's Republic of China instead. Second, he increased the war effort in Laos, forcing the North Vietnamese army to leave South Vietnam to protect their supply routes along

12 http://www.upi.com/News_Photos/News/Medal-of-Honor-awarded-to-MSGT-Richard-Etchberger/3849/

the Laos-Vietnamese border. This action relieved the pressure on the South Vietnamese army, making it appear they could handle the defense of their nation without US troops.

The Steve Canyon program, used USAF pilots called Ravens, in civilian clothes to pilot O1E light aircraft and to act as forward air controllers for the attack aircraft operating in Laos. The pilots had to be supplied with food, water, ammunition, and other essentials.

Ammunition for the Raven aircraft, which was mostly white phosphorous rockets for spotting, came from Pepper Grinder in Udorn, a munitions depot located near Udorn, Thailand. The ammunition was loaded on US military transports by US military personnel, and then flown by Air America pilots to outlying fields in Laos where the Ravens were located.

Air America began receiving more equipment from the military, including C-123 aircraft, modified to the K model, which incorporated two jet engines for better performance. Bell HU1D helicopters were also provided, as well as turbine-engine modifications to four of the H-34s. In addition, CH-47C heavy-lift helicopters were sent to Air America from the army. The fixed-wing lineup in the Vientiane group now included US Air Force C-130 transports and turbine-engine Twin Otters.

C-123K. Photo used by permission of Tom Lum.

C-130. Photo used by permission of Tom Lum.

Twin Otter. Photo used by permission of Tom Lum.

As such, Air America was instrumental in ending the Vietnam conflict and was used by the president of the United States specifically for that purpose. Air America afforded Nixon the military presence he needed in Laos while at the same time enabling him to make it appear to the rest of the world as if the United States were following the restrictions of the 1962 Geneva Accords. Without Air America, Nixon's "Vietnamization" program likely would have failed. You can find out more about the Vietnamization program at this referenced website.[13]

Nixon still had another problem, however. He needed to know what the North Vietnamese were thinking to obtain an edge at the bargaining table in Paris. Once again, he turned to Air America for the solution.

Air America had two H-500 helicopters used in Laos, but they were in fact only covers for two H-500P helicopters, which each cost more than one million 1972 dollars. The 500P had an extra rotor blade and a tail rotor that was altered to make less noise. Its engine had a muffler, as well, prompting it to be called the quiet helicopter.

LORAN ground navigation systems were a relatively new concept in those years, as were terrain-following radar and forward-looking infrared radar, sometimes referred to as "thermal imaging" and commonly called FLIR. The two 500P aircraft were outfitted with FLIR, an elaborate configuration that used liquid nitrogen. From the pilot's perspective, the FLIR consisted of a television monitor that displayed objects according to heat, so that images appeared as negatives. The pilot could discern the shape of a person, for example, by his body heat, but was unable to determine the identity. A car could be seen only if it had been recently driven and was still warm. Flying with the monitor was a challenge. A blade of grass looked like a tree on the monitor when the craft was parked on the ground. The pilot tended to go backward involuntarily when coming to a hover because the pilot's involuntary response was to keep back of any large object. It wasn't large of course, but it looked huge in the monitor. It took a lot of practice to overrule the brain.

The Vinh Tap Mission used the 500P to go into North Vietnam with a crew to splice into the main phone line. Crewmembers would place a series of antennas that resembled spider webs into trees, in locations where the telephone signals could be relayed from antenna to antenna, and finally to a place where the resulting telephone conversations could be monitored in safety. The Twin Packs were to act as SAR teams for the 500P on this mission. Two Twin Otter aircraft equipped with Terrain Following Radar were used in the mission as well. The LORAN navigation system, which is commonplace now, was relatively new in this era. It was amazing to us to be able to find

13 http://en.wikipedia.org/wiki/Vietnamization

objects as small as a paper wrapped tree in the middle of the night. Pilots were equipped with night goggles and learned to fly with them so that they could place intelligence-gathering teams in small landing zones without the use of lights.

Several weeks of intensive training were required to learn how to place the antenna in a tree while flying with night goggles. With the goggles on you couldn't see the instruments, and flying was strictly by feel and visual reference. The goggles still needed some light, and on a moonless night you had to strain to see objects. You could turn on the aircraft lights when landing, which were covered with infrared lenses. That way no one could see the lights from the outside.

The result of this elaborate secret mission: Air America fulfilled its responsibility for furnishing information to the American negotiators at the Paris peace talks, which allowed the US government to obtain a final peace plan and secure the release of the POWs held in Hanoi.

Seeking Recognition

The company, the mission, and the work ended, but a kindred spirit had developed among Air America employees. It's simply not possible to work together in a war zone for years and not develop relationships. For many of us, it was impossible to just let go of all that had happened, and so, through the efforts of several former employees, the Air America Association was established.

Initially, it was merely a social gathering, but it grew legs, and—to be meaningful—it needed character. A bronze memorial plaque was struck with all the names of those who had died in the quarter century of Air America's existence. The plaque was dedicated and delivered to the University of Texas at Dallas in a solemn ceremony among friends and relatives of the deceased on May 30, 1987. President Ronald Reagan sent his blessings. Jerry Fink, former deputy legal counsel for Air America, gave a moving eulogy, and acclaimed historian William Leary provided historical information about the company.

Sometime later, a brilliant suggestion was made to provide the University of Texas at Dallas with documents, papers, pictures, and memorabilia from the individual collections of former employees. At the time, no one realized how significant or huge the combined collection would become. Texas Tech University, who'd developed the Virtual Vietnam Archive, offered their expertise in the form of oral histories and their own archive. Annual reunions were organized, and a quarterly newsletter made former employees proud of their service and accomplishments.

But not all of the developments were positive. Many books were written, but there were many discrepancies, and the real truth about Air America was obscured. Certain books provided a slanted view of the company, providing historical distortions or outright misinformation. The truth was further clouded by a 1990 comedy movie starring Mel Gibson, which portrayed the company and its employees as a collection of psychotic misfits and criminals. Needless to say, those of us who knew the real Air America were disturbed by these misrepresentations.

Shortly after Air America Inc. was dissolved in 1976, it was publicly revealed that the CIA had owned the corporation. Apparently, this revelation was supposed to explain everything. In reality, it revealed nothing. Further, it's incredibly difficult to question the Central Intelligence Agency; for common citizens, it may even be impossible. So, despite the supposedly great revelation, the truth remained hidden.

Of course, that didn't stop former Air America employees from seeking justifiable benefits that were and have been denied.

Roy Watts, a former Air America employee, decided to seek disability benefits for a serious medical condition. According to Watts, a CIA attorney told him that he (Watts) had been handsomely rewarded as a highly paid mercenary, had enjoyed a tax-free haven, had known the risks, and should, therefore, accept the consequences.

In a completely separate case, Jerry Fink worked with a group of former company employees in an attempt to obtain benefits. To do so, they tried for years to classify their work with Air America as federal employment. As it was, if an Air America employee had five years with the company, the granting of that employment term as civil service credit would give him federal retirement benefits. The amount of the retirement annuity would be based upon the length of service, so an employee could increase his annuity amount by including any additional federal employment with another government agency. Military service time could also be counted, if the employee was not already receiving military retirement payments for that time. Jerry's group only needed the CIA to acknowledge their employment. But the CIA made no such admission.

Several years later, Watts presented his employment history to the courts and the Merit Systems Protection Board (MSPB), once again seeking federal benefits. The MSPB ruled against Watts, but a circuit judge said the issue should be presented to the United States Federal Court of Appeals. Thus, the cases of Fink, Hickler, and Watts were consolidated and presented together in federal court.

The ruling from the Federal Court of Appeals can be compressed into a single statement: "They had not been informed that they were in the federal retirement system at the time of their hiring, and their pay had not been docked accordingly. Therefore, they could not be classified as federal employees."[14]

It is probably presumptuous for me to find fault with a federal appellate court decision, but I strongly believe that the court erred. The US government owns a number of corporations, including the US Postal Service, the Tennessee Valley Authority, and Radio Free Europe. I have spoken at length with employees of all three of these corporations. None of their employees are enrolled in the federal retirement system, but all are entitled to federal benefits and protection. Each of these corporations has an employee retirement and benefit provision. Each of these corporations also provides health care for its employees, including disability and survivor benefits.

More importantly—and this is crucial in my opinion—each employee of these government-owned corporations is advised of his or her rights under the corporation's retirement plan and provided with advice regarding his or her benefits through a Health and Human Services department. In short, every employee of these government-owned corporations knows exactly who they are working for and for what benefits they are eligible.

Air America did have a retirement program, but it was ancillary, and not part of the employment package. It was an investment program with limited value, and most Air America personnel were never enrolled. And to the best

---

14 Roy F. Watts, Petitioner vs. Office of Personal Management, Respondent. *Appeal No. 85–2435.* United States Court of Appeals Federal Circuit. April 1, 1987.

of my knowledge, there was no Health and Human Services department to provide assistance or guidance, or even to answer basic questions.

Air America employees were also covered by workmen's compensation, but were not made aware of this benefit to my knowledge. Any company contracted with the US government is insured under workmen's compensation, but the average employee never saw these contracts or was even aware of them. If an Air America employee received an on-the-job injury that resulted in long-term disability, the settlement process was conducted secretly. No other employee was informed of the outcome. In other words, there was no provision for long-term care or compensation. For those who did so much, they received so little in return. The secrecy was intended to fool the public. It did more than that. It fooled the employees as well.

Whenever an employee died, his family was quickly packed up and sent out of the country, without any advice whatsoever in regard to seeking compensation. Some of the surviving wives, in fact, had to seek expensive legal assistance just to get what should have been automatically provided to them.

For all these reasons, I think the Federal Court decision should be revisited, but federal appellate courts rarely revisit their rulings, and attempting an appeal to the Supreme Court would most likely be futile.

The Air America Association does not have power of attorney to act on any former employee's behalf, but it does act to pursue benefits for former employees collectively, and it works to keep those former employees informed.

When president of the Association in the early 2000s, I approached Jerry Fink and suggested that we seek veteran status as an alternative to recognition as former federal employees.

Jerry agreed, declaring, "Half a loaf is better than none."

I brought the issue before the general membership at one of the annual reunions, and it was agreed to pursue veteran status. However, no one knew how to proceed. Leigh Coleman-Hotujec, a daughter of one of the pilots killed in action in Laos, suggested that we search for historical records tying Air America to military activity. She was sure that such records existed. We developed a plan of action accordingly, but shortly thereafter, former employee

Jesse Walton suggested we delay our pursuit of veteran status and approach Congress with a plea to have the federal decision overturned.

I disagreed with Walton's recommendation but quickly ran into opposition. I should mention that Walton worked as a line pilot for Air America from 1959 until it ended in Laos in 1974. It was his recommendation to start the Air America website, which I followed up with, and he is well-respected among his peers, serving with honor as the association's historian. Yet on this specific issue, I disagreed.

The opposition's argument was that veteran status would not provide tangible benefits. Many members were hoping for retirement benefits, and were afraid that veteran status would kill any possibility of ever receiving them. Also, most of Air America's flight crews were former military pilots, so they were already entitled to veterans benefits. I certainly couldn't disagree with their arguments, but then I was more interested in the intangible benefit of veteran status. Air America employees had been publicly characterized as mercenaries, drug runners, and psychotic misfits. That image was false, and receiving official recognition as military veterans would go a long way toward erasing the false impression. Further, several employees were not former military. Attaining veteran status would provide them with the healthcare benefits that they deserved and could not obtain otherwise.

I didn't see any reason to limit us to one strategy or the other, however. Why not pursue veteran status *and* ask Congress to overturn the decision of the federal court? There was definitely a precedent for such a move: the women service pilots of World War II had previously been awarded veteran status and eligibility for Civil Service Retirement (CSR). Their struggle for recognition had been long and difficult, but they had ultimately won.

So I favored trying both avenues. However, I didn't think it would be a good idea to pin all of our hopes on Congress. Several years earlier, a former Air America employee had asked his congressman to write to the CIA, requesting confirmation of his employment dates with the agency. He, justifiably, wanted to add his Air America time to his military time hoping he could accumulate enough time for retirement compensation.

The CIA response stated, "As you are aware, the Merit Systems Protection Board and the federal courts have consistently taken the position that employment by Air America was not an appointment to the Federal Civil Service, and the employee is not entitled to benefits or credits."

As far as the congressman was concerned, his work was done. He had written the letter and received an answer. No further action was required. Perhaps it didn't occur to him that the CIA's response might not be legally correct. He didn't ask for proof of any kind. He didn't even ask for a legal opinion from a second source. He accepted the CIA's statement at face value and gave the matter no further attention. I had a strong suspicion that any request we sent to Congress would receive the same treatment. We'd get a few friendly smiles, maybe a letter or two, and the matter would be dropped, with no real action.

My opponents' response to my recommendation not to pursue our goals through Congress was lukewarm. So I suggested sort of a compromise. I would write a letter to the CIA, asking for support and guidance. If my letter went unanswered, I would drop the issue of veteran status. The opponents agreed, so I sent a letter to the director of the Central Intelligence Agency, George Tenet. I didn't really expect a reply.

To my surprise, in April of 2003, I received a letter on CIA letterhead. It was from Mr. Martin C. Petersen, deputy executive director of the Central Intelligence Agency. He provided me with the address of the Civilian/Military Service Review Board (C/MSRB), whom he identified as the appropriate authority for veteran status applications. He further stated that if the Secretary of the Air Force, the executive agent for the reviewing board, or any other Department of Defense (DOD) official requested verification of facts relevant to the application, the agency would respond in the appropriate manner. A copy of DOD Directive 1000.20, which explains the application process, was attached.

Now it was official. Under the agreement reached with the opponents to seeking veteran status, the Air America Association was now supporting both issues. I went to work on the application, conducting research and doing a lot of writing.

The application for veteran status consisted of the CIA endorsement, testimonials, copies of USAF contracts, and other historical documents to support our position. The next step was for the C/MSRB to accept the application, indicating that it had merit for consideration. The C/MSRB did accept it but responded with a list of twenty questions, all printed on paper with "United States Department of the Air Force" letterhead. They wanted details concerning operational authority, names of directors, and specific contract information that I did not have in my possession but that I knew should be readily available at the Central Intelligence Agency. Based on the instructions in my previous letter from the CIA official Martin C. Petersen, I sent Martin a copy of the letter and asked for their support.

I received a very terse reply on CIA letterhead from a Mr. Robert A. Rebelo, chief human resources officer, stating that he was responding to my letter to Petersen. Rebelo noted that Petersen had indicated the CIA would respond, as appropriate, should the Secretary of the Air Force or any other Department of Defense official request the CIA's verification of facts relevant to the application. Rebelo's letter also informed me that, "The Agency has received no such request from the secretary of the air Force, or other appropriate Department of Defense official. Please understand that the Agency does not intend to respond to individual queries concerning this matter."

Alarmed, I responded to the C/MSRB with a request that they go directly to the CIA for the required information. The C/MSRB replied that it was not their responsibility to gather evidence. I pointed out that we were dealing with the CIA, and suggested that the board might make an exception in this case. The C/MSRB agreed and took the information request directly to the CIA. When all of the polite language was stripped away, the CIA essentially said no to them as well, by stating that it would take two years or more to answer their questions.

I refused to quit. For the next five years, I researched the history of Air America, conducted interviews, and wrote volumes of data. Finally, I was able to get the application in a condition whereas the executive secretary to the secretary of air force determined it merited review by the C/MSRB.

The application failed on a three-to-one vote. This was a crushing defeat for me, but almost immediately thereafter, the executive secretary for the

Secretary of the air force strongly urged me to resubmit the application, citing two books that had recently been brought to their attention.[15] [16]

I did so and took it a step further. Though I initially believed the CIA had owned Air America, just as everybody was telling us, doubt was beginning to creep in. Looking back on my experiences, I realized that I hadn't seen the connection then, and my only association between the two entities now was the result of what others had told me. Further, after reading the books the C/MSRB recommended along with several others, I noticed that the lines between the dots were not always being connected whenever the CIA's "secret airline" was being discussed. Namely, I noticed that some authors would interject the CIA when talking about Air America, with no attribution for the connection, as if it were cut and dried. Other authors, including those of very good books, seemed to add the term *CIA* in their discussions of Air America solely for sensationalism, and not as historical fact.

As I reflected further and tried to connect the dots, I realized that the CIA was a customer, but not the only customer. In Udorn, Air America had had an office building on the airport and so had the CIA. The CIA building had been referred to as AB-1. The buildings were not connected, and pilots did not go to AB-1 unless invited, which was rarely. We knew the CIA case officers up-country but were not personal friends with them. Our business was always professional. We did not mingle on our days off either. Even to this day, the case officers in Laos, commonly known as the SKY group—based on the fact that their activity was concentrated on Skyline Ridge, which rested alongside LS-20A in Laos—have their own social organization with biannual reunions. Occasionally, officers and board members of the Air America Association are invited to these, but never all of Air America.

The SKY group is a unique collection of individuals with harrowing experiences, including those in Laos, under their belts, all of which could

15 Warren A. Trest, *Air Commando One: Heinie Aderholt and America's Secret Air Wars,* Washington DC: Smithsonian Books, 2000.

16 Capt. Earl H. Tilford, Jr.: *Search and Rescue in Southeast Asia, 1961–1975.* Office of Air Force History, United States Air Force, 1980.

make very good stories; however, most of those individuals have elected to remain silent, with just a couple exceptions.[17]

Years later it was revealed Air America did have some imbedded CIA employees, but only a few, and they were paid on a different basis and taxed as if they lived in the United States. Most of them were contract employees initially but went on to become staff employees and, as such, were enrolled in the government's retirement plan.

In all of this, the realization I had was that the CIA employees in Laos knew who they worked for and had a clear understanding of their job descriptions and retirement benefits. On the other hand, Air America employees were neither fish nor fowl, as references to the CIA owning Air America appear to be in name only, with no apparent authority or jurisdiction. Further evidence of this realization ensued.

Several years after 1975, the CIA acknowledged Air America with a Unit Citation,[18] but it was a closed event. The Air Force, Army, and Navy essentially all said that we just happened to be in the area.

---

17 James E. Parker Jr.: Codename Mule: *Fighting the Secret War in Laos for the CIA*. Naval Institute Special Warfare 1995.

18 http://www.air-america.org/About/Citation_Medallion_Cachet.shtml

Support And Denial

Several former employees and military personnel who knew the truth about Air America wrote letters supporting the veteran status effort. Perhaps the letter from Hugh Grundy, then a grand old gentleman past ninety years of age, revealed what Air America was about more poignantly than any other person. Hugh Grundy wrote,

> From the time of its secret purchase, in about 1950, from commercial, profit-seeking owners, until its dissolution in the mid-seventies, when it was perceived as no longer needed after the Vietnam War ended, the CAT/Air America complex was owned by the United States government, administered through its Central Intelligence Agency. True ownership was classified and veiled by typical corporate structures with captive shareholders. True ownership was first revealed, I believe, in Mr. Nelson Rockefeller's Report to the President and later publicly by the CIA at a joint CAT/Air America reunion in Las Vegas in 2001. The only reason for existence of the CAT/Air America complex after that secret purchase was to serve government needs, especially its covert undertakings, not just to operate airlines as a profit-seeking business venture. It was projected and managed to only produce enough profit to be self-supporting in operations and buy its needed aircraft, equipment, and facilities, thusly

> relieving any need of subsidy. From late 1955 onward that goal was achieved and, in effect, gave the American taxpayer a free ride for services of the complex. During that period several millions of dollars of involuntary profits beyond need were voluntarily returned to Defense and upon dissolution. I understand some twenty-five million was turned over to Treasury.

Mr. Grundy went on to say, "CAT/Air America offered Government a means of conducting vital activities that, due to political or other restraints, could not employ military forces in the usual manner, and CAT/Air America sometimes substituted for a military presence and often worked hand-in-hand with the military, especially in covert operations."

In order to authenticate my application for veteran service, I needed documented proof for the many rescues of downed military personnel in Laos, and this proof needed to show that Air America operated under the jurisdiction and authority of the US military. I had my own experiences, of course, and letters from other former employees, but none of us had exact details that included the crewmember's names and the call signs of the aircraft that had been forced down. I also needed definite nexus between the military and Air America in written form. The logical places to find all this were at the Air Force Archive at Maxwell Air Force Base and at the Army's Center for Military History.

James Johnston, the executive secretary for the Secretary of the Air Force, contacted both and requested information that would corroborate my claim. Their responses were incredible. Both said there was no known evidence available to show that Air America was ever involved in military activity in Laos.

I showed copies of their letters to retired Major General Richard Secord, and he wrote a seething letter to the Civilian/Military Service Review Board telling them he had been the officer in charge of the Site 85 radar-site project and knew firsthand about Air America's involvement and designation as a joint SAR force along with the USAF.

I also contacted the Air Force Archive and asked, "What in the hell is going on with you people?" I was informed by e-mail that they were not allowed to discuss Air America, but that if I used some key words I could find what I wanted at Texas Tech University's Vietnam Archive. The key words were "Site 85" and "CHECO," which I found out meant Contemporary Historical Examination of Current Operations. In fact, you can Google those key words and find that report immediately.

Air America is scarcely mentioned in the information I found, but you can get a glimpse of its involvement, which was far more extensive than that stated in the report. However, the report did prove the Air America/military connection.

What all of this really meant was that I could obtain the information, but, unless the US government verified it publicly, the connection never existed, at least not officially.

Digging deeper in the Johnson Presidential Library, I was able to obtain telegrams between the ambassador in Laos, the Department of State, and the Department of Defense. These messages readily explained the complexity each were faced with, trying to honor their commitment to the 1962 Geneva Accords while not losing the war in Laos at the same time.

The following is a telegram that was declassified and placed in the Johnston Presidential Library.

> *Telegram from the Embassy in Laos to the Department of State*
> *Vientiane, May 24, 1964, 5:00 p.m.*
>
> *Source: Department of State, Central Files, POL 27 LAOS. Secret; Immediate. Repeated to Bangkok, CINCPAC, London, and Paris. Received at the Department of State at 8:17 a.m., May 24 and passed to the White House, JCS, OSD, CIA, and USUN at 4:30 p.m.*
>
> *Want Dept be fully aware of degree to which we now becoming involved in measures in violation Geneva Accords but which are absolutely necessary if we are to meet urgent requirements in this ugly situation.*
>
> *Souvanna called me on telephone this morning regarding threatening situation around Muong Kheung-Ban An-Muong Soui and asked for T-28 strikes in area. I told him [1 line of source text*

not declassified] to do anything quickly we would have to turn to US pilots for combat missions. Souvanna hesitated at first but finally gave me green light to proceed with US pilots. Accordingly I am authorizing US pilots (Air America civilians) to undertake T-28 flights tomorrow for two purposes: 1) help to hold PL advance on Ban An-Muong Soui area (Muong Kheung has reportedly now been evacuated); 2) Pilots will be briefed very carefully on known enemy dispositions and AA batteries. On a selective basis I am relaxing certain long-standing prohibitions: 1) Air America, particularly choppers, being permitted to carry military personnel in hill areas and also war material; 2) Dept already aware presence here US T-28 technicians; 3) closer ARMA and AIRA participation with FAR and RLAF in targeting for T-28 strikes and more direct USAID/RO participation in supply arrangements.

At same time Department appears nervous about any acknowledgment that Air America involved in maintenance T-28s in Udorn even though we have had to use Air America planes liberally in moving troops and munitions to and from areas such as Ban Na and Muong Soui where there are no aircraft which Lao can fly which can do the job.

The additional airlift aircraft (three C-123 and three Caribou), estimated by the Ambassador to be required (Vientiane to State 1694, 25 June 1964), /3/ can be made available from PACOM resources with no appreciable effect on the air effort in South Vietnam. When the requirement has been firmly established, the Joint Chiefs of Staff will direct CINCPAC to lend these aircraft to Air America at Udorn and to support them as required.

4. We are prepared to furnish additional T-28s promptly [1-1/2 lines of source text not declassified] we do not believe US civilian pilots required for T-28s in support of operation. However, US is prepared to use existing Air America aircraft, provide additional three C-123s and three Caribou, and permit use of US civilian pilots to bring GM-16 up to Muong Soui and to provide continuing resupply of operation as required. (Our public and third-country position would be that the operation is mercenary Air America and not US Government and that, in any event, the operation relates directly to defense of Neutralist forces along lines para 3 above.) FYI: We also considering authorizing use of napalm if Souvanna requests and you approve, in support of this or any other operation and not merely in case major Communist attack as you have previously requested and we have authorized. End FYI.

Author note: the slang used in this telegram is for the most part self-explanatory; however, abbreviations can be found in the appendix or at this website: http://history.state.gov/historicaldocuments/frus1961-63v24/terms

The word "mercenary" in the telegram is particularly galling, and more egregious is the obvious fact that though Air America crews were not mercenaries, the State Department wanted us to *look* like mercenaries to the unsuspecting public.

I was almost finished with my research when *The War in Northern Laos 1954–1973* by Victor B. Anthony and Richard R. Sexton was declassified. The book is highly redacted but represents the smoking gun I was looking for. CAS, which was the code name for CIA, is mentioned regularly, but its covert operations were said to be separate from military operations, even though Air America supported both factions.

The CIA was involved with the Hmong and so really didn't need Air America to be flying military aircraft. The CIA still used them, of course, but it was really the US government that needed Air America inside military aircraft. This fact angered the military. They often felt we were involving ourselves in their war, not understanding how fearful the United States government was about, first, violating the Geneva Accords and, second, the American and international public finding out about it.

As a consequence, there was strong disagreement among all the stakeholders concerning tactics as well as a reluctance to share information. Military aircraft operating in Laos often did not know Air America was there to support them and provide vital local information concerning enemy positions, safe routes, and emergency landing spots. And, in some instances, this lack of knowledge could have cost military personnel their lives. I often observed military helicopters flying over enemy positions and getting shot at, when they should have selected a safer route. On one occasion, a large military helicopter crashed on a runway with no enemy activity simply because the pilot had thought he had to come in fast and furious to avoid being shot. To survive, all these pilots would have had to do was get briefed by an Air America pilot who had operated there for years—but normally whenever advice was offered, they refused with an attitude that said they didn't need help from some mercenary pilot.

Then in 2009, the University of Texas at Dallas hosted an event in which the CIA honored Air America for its many accomplishments, and especially noted its rescue work. But the compliment had come with a twist.

Dr. Timothy Castle, who hosted the event, is an extremely intelligent and articulate man. He had been a door gunner with the Air Force rescue force in Thailand and had conducted several rescues in Laos during the war. Later, he received his formal education and wrote two very good books.[19] [20] Those who knew Dr. Castle said that he was critical of Air America, essentially expressing the sentiment that we were nothing more than ambulance chasers interfering with the military's work. Dr. Castle once tried to get me to admit that we were paid large sums of money for our SAR work and that money was our motivation, but I assured him that such rumors were untrue. Later, he accepted an invitation to be the guest speaker at an Air America reunion, so I thought that he might have altered his opinion of us.

At the 2009 University of Texas event, however, it seemed that Castle was trying a different tactic, and it may have worked. Castle decided to praise Air America but described us as people who acted in accordance with what he called an "airman's bond." According to him, we acted solely out of a desire to assist soldiers in need, and did so with no obligation, no orders, and no jurisdiction.

I was able to read a prelude of his presentation before the event, and I called

---

19 Timothy N. Castle, At War in the Shadow of Vietnam: *U.S. Military Aid to the Royal Lao Government, 1955–1975,* Columbia Press 1993

20 Timothy N. Castle, *One Day Too Long,* New York, Columbia Press 1999

him and asked him not to give the speech he had prepared. If he followed through with his planned presentation, it could damage or even destroy any chance for Air America pilots to receive future benefits, including civil service retirement or veteran status. Castle was completely unresponsive to my request. He said he hoped we could have a gentlemen's disagreement on this issue.

Worse, Castle asked me not to bring up anything controversial, and I didn't, although the event itself was structured in a manner that made it difficult to ask pointed questions.

Finally, in the fall of 2009, efforts by those seeking federal retirement benefits came to a head. Thanks to some work by Senator Harry Reid and Congresswoman Shelley Berkley, of Nevada, the 2010 Intelligence Authorization Bill included a requirement for the director of National Intelligence to report to the US Senate Select Committee on Intelligence about the history of Air America, and the feasibility of obtaining federal benefits for company employees. The bill became law in October 2009, and the director of National Intelligence (DNI) had six months to prepare a report.

The director resigned on almost the exact date the Air America report came due, after which a deputy sent a letter to the Senate Select Committee on Intelligence, essentially saying that the required report had not been completed. The deputy's letter repeated the often-stated declaration that the courts had already ruled on the issue of federal benefits for Air America personnel and promised follow-up reports every ninety days, if any new information should become available.

As of July 2011, it would appear that the current crop of officials in the intelligence community either didn't know the history of Air America, or simply didn't care, as the report had yet to be presented to Congress, even though the requirement was signed into law.

In August 2011, however, the DNI report was finally released, although, essentially, the report used the argument presented previously. Also, as I expected, the report presented Tim Castle's "airman's bond" theory as if it were an honor to Air America, but still stated that we acted without jurisdiction or authority, which is patently false. The report also stated that the museum at CIA headquarters, as an honor to the company, held several paintings reflecting Air America deeds, and it suggested that former employees should respect the homage. The report did not say that it was the members of the Air America Association who paid for the paintings and donated them to the museum. I guess you could say the former employees furnished our own honor and were now being asked to respect what we had done and not ask for anything more.

In my opinion, the CIA and Department of Defense are both hoping that the problem be eventually forgotten. They can't eliminate all inquiries, but, by issuing erroneous statements and shuttling the issue back and forth between them, they can probably prevent any hope of constructive action. If they keep the lid on the pot long enough, eventually all interest will fade, and people will stop asking the difficult questions.

The application for reconsideration of veteran status was turned down by the same three-to-one margin. This time it took more than six months before the decision was provided to me, and like the first time it was signed by an interim secretary of the Air Force who couldn't possibly have had time to read and digest all of the information contained inside. I was sure he simply rubber-stamped the board's decision.

I began to see a pattern emerging. After talking to other applicants who had been disapproved, I realized that the C/MSRB was never going to approve any organization, except for those that had operated during World War II, which were comprised of veterans who were too old to take advantage of the veteran status. Still, in one notable case, the Merchant Marines, with financial backing from the AFL/CIO, filed a legal suit that racked up more than a million dollars in legal expenses. They received only partial approval, but the decision did show the board had erred.

I could file suit, likewise, and I believe our complaint would be similar and have equal merit to the Merchant Marine suit, but I don't have a million dollars, and I don't have the backing of the AFL/CIO. So the issue appears to be dead.

I had attempted to get the president involved with my quest for veteran status several years earlier, and was met with the same stonewall tactics by senior Department of Defense officials. I found it appalling that one cannot get information and requests for assistance to the president without first going through certain unidentified Department of Defense officials, who, on their own, decide whether an issue warrants the president's attention. I realize the president can't see everybody's wish list, but was not aware that the screening process involved the Department of Defense. Regardless, the DOD told my emissary that the CIA was the venue to approach with this issue, since they were the owners of the company. Now knowing that claim is false, I find it difficult to believe that senior DOD officials do not know the truth. The DOD also said that, if Air America were to be recognized, the door would be opened for other civilian organizations doing similar work, and that would be counterproductive.

Not true. It would depend on how the civilian company was structured. There were two other major companies that operated in Laos other than Air America. Continental Air Services and Bird & Sons also had contracts with the government. Their work environment was for the most part equally hazardous and nothing said here should belittle that effort, but there were distinct differences. CASI and Bird & Sons' employees were under the jurisdiction of their respective board of directors and neither company operated military aircraft that were not FAA certified. Further, neither company was designated, or charged with SAR responsibility and were not involved with paramilitary activity by direction. The employees of these two companies certainly conducted noble work, and Bird & Sons employee Ernest Brace was captured and held as a prisoner of war for eight years, but he was not a combatant. CASI and Bird & Sons could leave the area with all of their equipment at the whim and caprice of their board of directors.

Air America did not have this autonomy and remained at the discretion of the president of the United States regardless of the situation. The difference between Air America and these other companies regarding benefits and veteran status recognition is jurisdiction, and in that respect Air America was uniquely different. The structure of Air America was probably a mistake that would never be repeated, but that mistake was at the expense of the employees.

So, in the end, the U.S. Government may deny honoring Air America, but we haven't yet given up hope. A reconsideration request to the Secretary of the Air Force was granted board review November 2012 based on two recent documents. *Operation Millpond: U.S. Marines in Thailand, 1961* by USMC Col. George R. Hofmann Jr. and *The United States Air Force in Southeast Asia: The War in Northern Laos, 1954-1973* by Victor Anthony and Richard Sexton.

The first document supports the claim by former employees the U.S. Marine Corps supported Air America by establishing Air America's operations and maintenance facility at Udorn, Royal Thai Air Force Base and turned over their military H-34 helicopters to Air America to fly in Laos. The second document supports the claim by former Air America employees they supported the USAF in Laos logistically, while conducting SAR operations, and were under the authority and jurisdiction of the 7th/13th Air Force while doing so.

The reconsideration request is currently under review by the Civilian/ Military Service Review Board after more than one year of testimonials and rebuttals to international attorneys at the USAF JAO, who claim Air America employees were "unprivileged belligerents" and therefore not qualified for veteran status, and USAF and U.S. Army historians who claim Air America employees do not qualify because they were not integrated into the armed forces and were not under the jurisdiction of the Uniform Code of Military Justice.

Branding covert and clandestine operations and denying benefits to those who participated as unlawful combatants is normally an accusation made by the opposing force, in this case the NVA and Pathet Lao, and not by your own government. Technically, everybody conducting military operations in Laos was an unprivileged belligerent, including the USAF Ravens and the North Vietnamese Army, but the only group that did not receive benefits was Air America.

It was pointed out jurisdiction under the Uniform Code of Military Justice would be favorable, but it is not a strict requirement for recognition and none of the other recipients, including the AVG (Flying Tigers), WW2 Women Air Force Service Pilots, or the Merchant Marines met those requirements.

We hope and pray for a just ruling, but if denied again, it would be a bitter pill to swallow and honor unjustly denied.

I suppose the resulting empty feeling that all of us in the association likely have will remain forever, but I also know that, deep down inside, we also have pride in knowing that we saved lives and, perhaps, ultimately helped secure peace in the Pacific Rim.

After Dave Kendall disembarked from the *Blue Ridge* and was released from Air America, he flew from Hong Kong to Taipei and met with me looking for a job. I told him my position with Great China Airlines was tenuous at best. The contract with Gulf Oil was soon to expire and there were no other contracts available. I listened attentively about his last day in Saigon and the handling of the employees when they arrived in Hong Kong. There was no longer any doubt in my mind. Any chance of returning to Southeast Asia flying for the war effort was extinguished.

Shortly thereafter, I gathered up my family and returned to the United States. I settled in Louisiana. Lucette found a house and declared, "This is where I want to live." We've been here ever since. Like my father before me, I finally found where I belonged, and over the years the demons of war inside me began to subside.

Dave hired on with a helicopter outfit in Louisiana when he came back to the United States. On his days off, he commuted to Tennessee where Ruth and the kids lived. On one of his trips home, he was tragically killed in an automobile accident.

Years later, Ruth visited her sister in Chicago, where they dined at a Vietnamese restaurant. Ruth and her sister conversed with the owner, who was very proud of her business and her successful children, who had all been educated in America.

Ruth told her, "My husband used to work in Vietnam. He was a pilot for Air America."

The restaurant owner looked at Ruth intensely and slowly said, "You know, I was rescued from a rooftop in downtown Saigon on the last day. I will never forget the pilot. He didn't wear a uniform, like the others. He had a colored shirt and overalls."

Ruth gasped and tears welled in her eyes. "That was my husband, David," she said.

They all broke down in tears.

END

Acknowledgments

In the spring of 2008, I had the privilege of being invited to speak at a reunion of Air America dependents, which was to be held that summer in Dallas. The audience, I was told, wanted to hear positive things about their dads, and I wanted to make the best possible impression. It occurred to me that a truly good painting of the H-34 helicopter would be an appropriate touch to the speech, so I began searching the Internet for an aviation artist. Joe Kline's website, http://www.joekline.com, jumped off the page. I contacted Joe, and he agreed to paint the picture.

The value of an aircraft painting is only enhanced by its technical accuracy, so I sought assistance from Mr. Wayne Knight, who had been the chief helicopter pilot during my tenure with Air America. Wayne, a former marine, was one of the original H-34 pilots in Udorn, Thailand. Wayne's assistance with exact detail, coupled with Mr. Kline's artistic expertise, resulted in an historical masterpiece. The painting was unveiled at the reunion, where, exactly as I'd hoped, it wowed everyone who saw it.

Three duplicate prints were authorized, and, through an expensive and exhaustive process, they look almost exactly like the original. One print was shipped to Wayne, who now dwells in Australia, for his valuable assistance. Wayne was wounded in battle with Air America. Not seriously, but wounded nonetheless. As such, he, along with several other Air America employees, deserves the Purple Heart.

Dr. Larry D. Sall, former Dean of Libraries at the University of Texas at Dallas, accepted one print for the University's Air America collection. Dr.

Stephen F. Maxner, director of the Vietnam Center at Texas Tech University, accepted the final print for the center's collection. The original painting hangs in my office, with honor. Here, I also want to specifically mention my sincere thanks to Mr. Paul Oelkrug, CA, University of Texas at Dallas. All three of these gentlemen—Sall, Maxner, and Oelkrug—and both of these universities have spent years supporting former Air America employees, and hours and hours of dedicated work presenting Air America's history to the public. Had it not been for these fine men and all those who worked alongside them, much of the history of Air America would never have come to light. I hope that this book adds credit to their efforts, and I thank them sincerely from my heart.

I would also like to thank the following people for their assistance in making this book a reality: Marc Yablonka, author of *Distant War: Recollections of Vietnam, Laos, and Cambodia*, for encouraging me to personalize my Air America historical research; Tom Lum, for his advice and friendship, and for allowing me to use his personal photographs; Jeff and Maria Edwards of NavyThriller.com for their advice and editorial assistance; Martha Pogue-Gregory for her exhaustive research and editorial assistance with the letters to the C/MSRB; and all those who shared in my experiences with the Marines and Air America.

As always, however, my deepest debt of gratitude is to my wife, Lucette, for knowing when to back me up, when to kick me in the teeth, and when to let me gallop off in pursuit of some crazy idea.

Appendix I: Abbreviations

AID, Agency for International Development

ARMA, Army Attach

ARVN, Army of the Republic of Vietnam

CAT, Civil Air Transport CENTO, Central Treaty Organization

CHMAAG, Chief, Military Assistance Advisory Group

CHPEO, Chief, Programs Evaluation Office

CINCARPAC, Commander, United States Army, Pacific

CINCPAC, Commander in Chief, Pacific

CINCPACFLT, Commander in Chief, Pacific Fleet

COMUSMACV, Commander, United States Military Assistance Command, Vietnam

Confe, series indicator for telegrams to the United States Delegation at the Conference on Laos in Geneva

DCM, Deputy Chief of Mission

Deptel, Department of State telegram

Dir, Director

DNC, Democratic Neutralist Committee

DRV, Democratic Republic of Vietnam

FBIS, Foreign Broadcast Information Service

FM, Foreign Minister

FRC, Federal Records Center

ICC, International Control Commission

IO, Bureau of International Organization Affairs, Department of State

IMF, International Monetary Fund

ISA, Office of the Assistant Secretary of Defense for International Security Affairs

JCS, Joint Chiefs of Staff

JUSMAG, Joint United States Military Assistance Group

KMT, Kuomintang (Nationalist Party), Republic of China

L, Office of the Legal Adviser, Department of State

L/FE, Assistant Legal Adviser for Far Eastern Affairs

LP, Luang Prabang

LPK, Lao Political Party

LTAG, Lao Training Advisory Group

MA, Military Attach

MAAG, Military Assistance Advisory Group

NCO, Non-Commissioned Officer

NIE, National Intelligence Estimate

NLHX or NLHZ, Neo Lao Hak Xat (or Zat), the political arm of the Pathet Lao

NNC, Neutral Nations Commission

NSC, National Security Council

NVN, North Vietnam

OSD, Office of the Secretary of Defense

PACAF, Pacific Air Force

PARU, Police Aerial Resupply Unit

PDJ, Plaine des Jarres (Plain of Jars)

PEO, Programs Evaluation Office

PL, Pathet Lao

PM, Prime Minister

POLAD, Political Adviser

POW, Prisoner of War

RCT, Regimental Combat Team

RTAF, Royal Thai Air Force

RTG, Royal Thai Government

S, Office of the Secretary of State

SEA, Southeast Asia

SEATO, Southeast Asia Treaty Organization

Secto, series indicator for telegrams from the Secretary of State while away from Washington

SNIE, Special National Intelligence Estimate

SOV, Office of Soviet Union Affairs, Bureau of European Affairs, Department of State

SVN, South Vietnam

Tosec, series indicator for telegrams to the Secretary of State while away from Washington

UK, United Kingdom

UN, United Nations

UNGA, United Nations General Assembly

UPI, United Press International

USAF, United States Air Force

USG, United States Government

USOM, United States Operations Mission

USSR, Union of Soviet Socialist Republics

VM, Vietminh

XK, Xieng Khouang

Appendix II: Websites

1. Allen Cates Collections

   At the Vietnam Center and Archive. Search the archive at http://www.vietnam.ttu.edu/virtualarchive by going to "Advanced Search" and typing in "Allen Cates" as the collection name.

   At the McDermott Library, University of Texas at Dallas. Search "The Archives" and then search "Cates, Allen" at http://www.utdallas.edu/library/uniquecoll/speccoll/hac/cataam/cataa.html

2. Marine Medium Helicopter Squadron 365. http://www.angelfire.com/de/HMM365Vietnam

3. The Official A-1 Skyraider Website. http://skyraider.org

4. Lowell Pirkle. http://www.arlingtoncemetery.net/lpirkle.htm

5. The Loss of Spectre 22. http://www.jollygreen.org/Stories/DavidPreston/loss_of_specter_22.htm

6. Air America. http://www.air-america.org

CPSIA information can be obtained
at www.ICGtesting.com
Printed in the USA
LVHW081356250721
693629LV00019B/974